That's Life with Autism

of related interest

Homespun Remedies
Strategies in the Home and Community for Children with Autism Spectrum
and Other Disorders
Dion E. Betts and Nancy J. Patrick
ISBN 1 84310 813 5

Parenting Across the Autism Spectrum
Unexpected Lessons We Have Learned
Maureen F. Morrell and Ann Palmer
ISBN 1 84310 807 0

Voices from the Spectrum
Parents, Grandparents, Siblings, People with Autism, and Professionals Share
their Wisdom
Edited by Cindy N. Ariel and Robert A. Naseef
ISBN 1 84310 786 4

Parent to Parent
Information and Inspiration for Parents Dealing
with Autism or Asperger's Syndrome
Ann Boushéy
ISBN 1 84310 774 0

Talking Teenagers
Information and Inspiration for Parents of Teenagers
with Autism or Asperger's Syndrome
Ann Boushéy
ISBN 1 84310 844 5

**Achieving Best Behavior for Children
with Developmental Disabilities**
A Step-By-Step Workbook for Parents and Carers
Pamela Lewis
ISBN 1 84310 809 7

**Kids in the Syndrome Mix of ADHD, LD, Asperger's,
Tourette's, Bipolar, and More!**
The One Stop Guide for Parents, Teachers, and Other Professionals
*Martin L. Kutscher MD, with contributions from Tony Attwood PhD
and Robert R. Wolff MD*
ISBN 1 84310 810 0

Disorganized Children
A Guide for Parents and Professionals
Edited by Samuel M. Stein and Uttom Chowdhury
ISBN 1 84310 148 3

**Encouraging Appropriate Behavior for Children
on the Autism Spectrum**
Frequently Asked Questions
Shira Richman
ISBN 1 84310 825 9

That's Life with Autism

Tales and Tips for Families with Autism

*Edited by Donna Satterlee Ross
and Kelly Ann Jolly*

Jessica Kingsley Publishers
London and Philadelphia

First published in 2006
by Jessica Kingsley Publishers
116 Pentonville Road
London N1 9JB, UK
and
400 Market Street, Suite 400
Philadelphia, PA 19106, USA

www.jkp.com

Library of Congress Cataloging in Publication Data
That's life with autism : tales and tips for families with autism / edited by Donna Satterlee
Ross and Kelly Ann Jolly.
    p. cm.
Includes index.
ISBN-13: 978-1-84310-829-0 (pbk.)
ISBN-10: 1-84310-829-1 (pbk.)
  1. Autistic children--Family relationships. 2. Parents of autistic children. 3. Autism--Pa-
tients--Family relationships. 4. Autism in children. I. Ross, Donna Satterlee, 1972- II. Jolly,
Kelly Ann, 1968-   •
  RJ506.A9T43 2006
  618.92'85882--dc22
                        2006013539

British Library Cataloguing in Publication Data
A CIP catalogue record for this book is available from the British Library

ISBN-13: 978 1 84310 829 0
ISBN-10: 1 84310 829 1

Printed and bound in the United States by Thomson-Shore, Inc.

To Jamie, Kate and Rebecca—
mothers who know.
D.R.

In loving memory of H. Weston Hubbard,
Crystal Fuhrman and Gail Y. Liester.
You will continue on in our hearts and souls.
K.J.

Acknowledgments

We gratefully acknowledge the support
of our husbands, Jared and Bill, our children, Logan, Asa, Adria,
Jessica, Ryan, Thor and Shaelyn, and all those who
contributed to the stories in this book.

Contents

How to use this book

Something to Talk About sections are designed to help individuals understand the questions they should ask other parents and professionals they come into contact with. They are also for use in facilitating group discussions in support group meetings and classrooms.

Reflection Activities are designed to give the reader greater insight into where they are at personally in regards to each topic area.

Disclaimer

The stories in this book are based on personal experiences. Please consult a medical professional before using any treatment. The editors and contributors are not liable for any accident or injury that may occur.

Introduction

Out of the corner of my eye I noticed my husband's college newspaper lying open on the table. I skimmed the classified section with interest:

> My name is Sarah. I am 4 years old and have autism.
>
> Therapist needed for ABA program, flexible hours.
>
> No experience necessary (will train). $9/hour.

Little did I suspect that the decision to answer the advertisement would change my life as I knew it. To me, at first, it was just a part-time job to pay the bills and keep my foot in the door of my profession. I thought I could drive to work, spend a couple of hours doing drills that someone else created and go home to be with my new baby—no responsibilities beyond the front door, no strings attached. There was no contract and I could leave whenever I wanted.

By the end of my first week at work I was hooked. Helping Sarah taught me a whole new way of looking at the world. When I arrived I didn't know the first thing about autism. My knowledge was limited to a horrible black-and-white film from the 1960s that I had watched in an Abnormal Psychology class as an undergraduate; it included footage of a boy repeatedly banging his head on a wall. Thanks to Jamie, Sarah's mother, my limited vocabulary soon included terms like Lovaas, thimerosal and casein. Catherine Maurice became my hero, as I'm sure she did for many of you, too. I also learned the correct use of prompting, reinforcers, and restraints.

More importantly, though, I didn't just feel like an employee—I felt like a member of the family. Through our conversations at the beginning and end of each session Jamie grew to be like a mother, sister, best friend, educator and mentor rolled in to one. In return I listened to her concerns about the therapy program, the school system, and her hopes and fears for Sarah. With my limited experience dealing with autism I wished I could do more, but I didn't know how.

I spent the next two years doing everything I could to keep the program going and ensure that Sarah received consistent therapy at home. Thinking up new drills, training therapists and ultimately hiring other therapists were all part of my expanding duties. I watched as Jamie slowly removed herself from the program, increasingly overwhelmed by the stress, until one day the strain became too much and she left. No one told the therapists exactly what had happened but one thing was obvious: she was out of the picture, at least temporarily. After that the program fell apart and I also left.

After a six-month stint away from autism, and the birth of my second child, I felt compelled to return to work. I found a new family and started the process of investing myself in their program—professionally and emotionally—and I integrated myself into the rhythm of the family and therapy team. Again, I was struck by how much the mother relied on me to talk through concerns and simply to listen. While my knowledge had definitely increased, I still felt inadequately prepared to answer her questions in the breadth and depth she needed. Ultimately the family left the state to be closer to a specialized school; again, I felt that although I had performed my duties as a therapist, I hadn't done enough to help the mother.

Then an idea came into my mind. What if there was a book, written *for* parents, *by* parents who wanted to share their experiences with autism in order to help other parents who were experiencing similar trials? I set a goal to interview two parents in every state, but quickly determined I had bitten off more than I could chew. My personal contacts in the autism community were limited and centralized in one state. I needed help and I didn't know where to turn. So I did what most parents in this book suggest and tried my luck on the Internet. Immediately I connected with people across the country that were willing to help. Two treasured resources I discovered were the Parent 2 Parent Network at Unlocking Autism (www.unlockingautism.org) and the co-editor of this book, Kelly Jolly. I found Kelly through a discussion board at www.parenthoodplace.com, which she hosts and, based on the merit of her story (see "Kelly and Shaelyn" in Chapter 1) asked her to assist in collecting the stories for this book. She shared my vision to support the families of children diagnosed with autism.

This book is the end result of our passion and desire to help mothers and other family members to cope with autism in their lives. The original concept was to provide a forum for parents to help other parents, and to provide hope and healing; however, in the process of discovering the stories, it became so much more. Each story provides a unique look into "life with autism" but, more than that, the stories provide a basis for understanding common experiences, discussions, and personal reflection. This book is for you, as a testament to my love for those family members who sacrifice so much to make a difference in the life of a child.

Donna Satterlee Ross

1.

D-Day: Life Before, During, and After Diagnosis

Angela and Cody (7)

Last summer I took Cody and his younger brother Seth to the park to play. Cody's speech was improving and he was trying his best to make friends with the other kids, but they were not being very nice. One child even called Cody retarded. These kids were being downright mean to him but he still kept trying to talk to them and play with them. I kept redirecting him to play with his brother or by himself. Abruptly, Cody started yelling at me and telling me it was my fault he didn't have friends because I wouldn't let him play with the kids he wanted to play with. Cody proceeded to pick up a stick and said, "This is my best friend," and told me to leave him alone. Cody spent the rest of the day talking and playing with that stick. He treated that stick as if it were another kid.

Later that night, while I was making dinner, I noticed Cody was angrily poking himself in the eye. Self-injury was something we were used to, but not to this degree. I stopped what I was doing to calm him down. I was trying desperately to keep him from stabbing his eye out. The whole time I was fighting to stop him he was laughing at me. I asked Cody, "Why would you want to poke out your own eye? Don't you know that will hurt?" Out of his innocent little mouth came the words, "Because Mommy, then you take me to doctor and I be normal." That was the day I knew he understood he was different. I had hoped he would never understand that the world could be cold and cruel. Our kids understand way more than we give them credit for—even the stuff we don't want them to understand.

Cody was 17 months old when I realized he was different. He went from a happy-go-lucky, pleasurable baby, to a child who wanted nothing to do with the rest of the world. He had acquired a vocabulary of about 60 words but then he stopped speaking entirely. He would turn the TV up as loud as he could and beat himself in the head repeatedly until his father or I would stop him. He stopped looking at us and playing with us, and just sat and colored with a black crayon. If we tried to take him out of the house he would kick, scream, bite, and hit. Needless to say we didn't leave the house very much unless it was an emergency. Cody was constantly getting sick with colds, lung infections, asthma and a weird rash that he still gets sometimes. He was also plagued by ear infections and was routinely throwing up.

When I first figured out something was very wrong, I thought Cody might have had a brain tumor. Cody was so ill that we were in and out of the doctor's office several times a month. I asked the doctor why Cody was being so hard to handle and had stopped talking. The doctor simply said, "Welcome to the terrible twos a few months early!"

Over the next three years, I continued to ask this doctor and others what was wrong with my son; I heard comments like, "You are not strict enough with him. He doesn't have to talk because you do everything for him," and my all-time favorite, "*You are overreacting*, he is fine."

When Cody still was not speaking at age four and a half, it was undeniable that something was not normal. I had his father demand the doctor do something. On our behalf, the doctor contacted the Head Start unit of Dauphin County, Pennsylvania, and set up a meeting. At the interview a teacher spent all of 15 minutes with my son before saying to me, "I am not an expert but I think the boy has autism." I asked her how we could find a definite answer and she said, "I'll put his name in a big pile and when they get to his name they will call you for an evaluation." I didn't particularly care for that option, since it had already taken three years. When I asked about our other options she told me that if our health insurance covered it we could have him diagnosed privately. Fortunately, the insurance did cover it, so that is exactly what we did.

Four weeks after the meeting at Head Start we were sitting in the office of a psychologist at Hershey Medical Center. The doctor, an occupational therapist and a speech pathologist spent a combined total of about four hours with Cody before making a diagnosis. When we were called back in to talk about what they had found the psychologist kept referring to "these kids like Cody" over and over. Finally I spoke up and asked, "What do you mean 'kids like Cody'?" I will never forget the doctor's expression as long as I live. She looked me in the eye and said, "I am not sure your son has autism or if your son is just somewhere on the autism spectrum, but have you ever seen the movie *Rain Man?*" At that point I passed out and my ex-husband had to pick me up off the floor. After I recovered, we left the office with a piece of paper that stated the diagnosis of moderate to severe autism and possible mental retardation. I felt my life was over and, even worse, I felt like Cody's was over, too. It was not until that night, after I went home, got on the computer, and started hunting for information on autism, that I found some solace and hope.

In many ways it feels like my first son died and was replaced with another. The Cody I once knew is gone forever. I love him and miss him, and wonder what his life would have been like. I love the child he is now, but I know his life is always going to be a challenge. He will probably not play sports or be Mr. Popular. However, he is always going to be my son. Cody has come a long way from his original diagnosis in a very short period of time. His current level of functioning is very high and his diagnosis was changed this year to Pervasive Developmental Disorder-Not Otherwise Specified (PDD-NOS)/Obsessive-Compulsive Disorder (OCD)/Severe Global Apraxia/Anxiety Disorder. And, just so you know, his IQ is 105, which rules out the possibility of mental retardation as originally presumed.

Angela's tips

- Do not give up! Autism isn't the end of the world; it's just the beginning of a different one than you planned.

- Work with your child constantly. Repeat everything until it clicks.

- Fight for the services you think your child needs; you probably know more about what the child needs than teachers and school districts.

- Trust your instincts; no one knows your child like you do…even his doctors.

- Engage the child in your world by doing things with him even when he protests.

CR

Barbie and John Matthew (10)

I used to call John Matthew a "nervous Nellie" when he was little. He would worry non-stop. I would find myself going through scenarios for activities with him so he'd know what to expect. I rehearsed each upcoming situation and created a social story. For instance, if we were going to a birthday party, I'd tell him who was going to be there, what they were probably going to be doing, and that people would be coming up to him and he needed to say "Hi" or "Happy birthday" to them. Instinctively I felt that was what I needed to do with him. Now I know why. Back then I thought of these rehearsal routines as something all moms do to ensure their children will be okay.

Growing up, John Matthew was the perfect child. He didn't go through the terrible twos or the terrible threes. I remember all the other parents complaining about their children throwing fits and acting out, while John Matthew was perfectly content with the world. Then when he was two years old he had his first febrile seizure. We called an ambulance and he stayed in the emergency room for several hours until they released him.

In the week following his seizure, John Matthew began stuttering and he became angry about everything. He never had any temper problems or communication issues prior to that. Approximately every five or six months he'd get sick again for various reasons and end up with another fever. Within the first 24 hours of onset of the fever he'd have another seizure. Toward the end of the week after each seizure occurred the strange behavior would wane—the stuttering would lessen and he'd become his usual cheerful self. I remember taking him to the doctor and saying, "This is weird. Everyone says that febrile seizures are benign, but I see changes."

By the time John Matthew was four and a half he'd had eight seizures. Each time I expressed my concerns, but the doctors kept telling me there was nothing to worry about. Fortunately for us, his last seizure occurred in the parking lot of the doctors' office. I ran inside and yelled, "My son is having another seizure!" On that particular day, the doctor was new and totally freaked out that John Matthew was having a seizure. The staff got him out of our car and brought him into the office. The doctor asked, "How many of these has he had?" When I told him, he said, "Have you ever seen a neurologist?" I replied, "I've asked to see a neurologist for the past two years and everyone keeps telling me that the seizures are harmless and not to worry." Without hesitation the young doctor made the referral.

In Las Vegas there are only two pediatric neurologists, so by the time we saw the doctor John Matthew was acting very unusual. He wanted to be on the floor whenever he became nervous and had lots of odd behavior I'd never seen before. We went in strictly for an assessment on his febrile seizures. However, the neurologist also had John Matthew up on the table and was asking him to do things like put his arms straight up, bend his arms, and perform some follow-the-leader type activities. John Matthew was clearly having trouble with those. Next, the neurologist started asking me questions that had nothing to do with febrile seizures and I didn't have a clue where the procedure was heading. An hour later he had written down "Asperger's Syndrome" on a piece of paper and said, "Go look this up."

Also written on the paper was the name of a website, containing the word "autism." I thought, "That's weird. What does autism have to do with Asperger's Syndrome?" Returning home, I looked up Asperger's Syndrome on the Internet and it was like someone gave me the missing piece to a puzzle. As I read over the list of common characteristics I remember exclaiming to myself, "Ah ha! That is why he is so anxious. This is why he laughs inappropriately. That is why he can't ride a bike or balance on the seesaw." The information I discovered also explained why he still used parallel play with his friends and was slow to join in with activities. All the behaviors that seemed strange to me a moment before suddenly made sense—like looking through a camera while you focus it, everything became clear.

Barbie's tip

- Keep talking until somebody listens!

☙

Debbie and Greg (15)

Like all mommies-to-be, I was anxious and excited for the arrival of my first baby. Not liking surprises, I found out ahead of time that it was a boy. The baby room was prepared months in advance, and my hospital bag at the foot of the bed was ready to go! I was fully prepared to give birth and to begin enjoying motherhood. As I had mentioned, I don't like surprises, but as life would have it, surprises are inevitable. At what was to be my final prenatal visit, my doctor informed me I needed to have a C-section and scheduled it for that afternoon. I started to panic. My poor husband; I ordered him to take me to my parents' house first and then we went home to grab my bag before making the journey to the hospital.

At 2:55 p.m. on a winter day in January, I gave birth to an eight pound eight ounce boy. We named him Greg. He seemed perfect. It wasn't until he was six months old that I began noticing some autistic characteristics (although I didn't have a name for them at the time). I could never get him on any kind of consistent schedule. Whenever we went into stores with bright lights he became agitated and fussy. Sounds made him jump and he would startle very easily. Greg could be sound asleep and all of a sudden he would tense up, even without hearing a noise. This struck me as being very odd. I knew his lack of eye contact was not normal either. I tried to engage him in play-related activities to gain his attention, but failed.

Before Greg I was what you would consider a scheduled individual. Although I tried I could never get him on a consistent feeding or sleep schedule. To say that he was a hard-to-read baby is an understatement! Adding to my frustration Greg had only a couple of foods he liked to eat. He was extremely sensitive to certain fabrics, too.

At three years old Greg still used single words rather than sentences to communicate, and did a great deal of babbling. He became very agitated when he could not express himself verbally and I knew deep down this was not just a speech delay. His preschool teacher, who was certified in special education, advised me to contact Early Child Intervention (ECI). The screening at ECI also indicated delays, but no one mentioned the "A word" just yet.

Greg attended ECI three times a week for services. While he was in sessions, I would sit in the next room looking at all the books on autism that lined the wall. In the meantime, ECI had come up with a possible diagnosis, autism, but I thought Greg was still too young for that to become official. At ECI, I was introduced to a wonderful developmental pediatric doctor. Impressed with her credentials, I brought Greg in to her office for a formal evaluation. Every test available was given to him. His IQ measured in the superior range. The bad news: he was autistic. The good news: he was very high functioning.

Today my wonderful son is in high school and never ceases to amaze us. Greg is an inspiration to many people and even takes advanced classes in math and science. He maintains an A average and was recently inducted into the National Honor Society. He also plays in the high school marching band and his other accomplishments are many. While he doesn't have a wide array of friends, he does not shy away from activities. He has gained so much confidence by living life to the fullest.

Debbie's tips

- Begin early intervention as soon as possible.

- Have evaluations done outside the school to give you a different perspective.

- Keep a journal to record in daily. I still have mine.

- Organize folders for easy access to information: Individualized Education Program (IEP) meeting notes, school records, medical records and one for extracurricular activities.

- Become an advocate for yourself, as well as for your child.
- Don't isolate yourself. Find a support group.

CR

Janis and Jared (6)

I am a special education teacher, but to be honest, I didn't realize there was anything wrong with Jared until he turned three. Now that I look back, and I have learned more specifically about autism, the signs were unmistakable. He definitely had communication, emotional, social, and behavioral problems. Yet, after 18 years of working with inarticulate children every day, I had no problem understanding small children with speech impairments. I could understand him where someone else probably couldn't. In hindsight, I recognize a lot of things were happening way before he was three. He acted deaf. He would run off and have no fear of danger. I would yell, "*Stop!*" and chase him; he would keep running. When I would finally catch him and explain, "Stop means stand still," he would laugh, without any recognition or understanding.

Jared has always had a gift for reading and a knack for visual and spatial tasks. He started talking at ten months. At a year and a half, he could take all the videos out of their boxes and then match them up correctly again. I have recordings of him doing 50-piece puzzles when he was three. So even considering the behaviors I mentioned before, it never crossed my mind to worry about Jared. Since my younger son, Dylan, had a traumatic birth experience and chronic ear infections I took him to the Alaska Center for Children and Adults to receive Project TEACH services. I wanted to make sure he was developmentally on track because he had had such serious problems as an infant. When they asked me if I had any concerns about my older son I said, "Oh no, he's smart."

Jared seemed so intelligent to me and started doing things so young that his development was never an issue. There were signs of regression, though. We started attending Kindermusik when he was a year old. He always loved the singing, dancing, and music, but one day out of the blue he just completely stopped participating. Instead of joining in the fun with the rest of the kids he started running around the group screaming. The evidence was mounting, but we ignored it.

Another blatant example that something was wrong occurred when Jared was two and we made the seven-hour drive to Anchorage from our home, stopping every couple of hours to let the kids run around. When we got to the hotel room it was late but Jared started flying around the room like the Tasmanian Devil. He was running on the beds, jumping everywhere, until finally we had to restrain him. When we did, his legs kept spinning in the air and I remember my husband shouting, "*This is not normal!*"

I also recall a fateful trip around that time to a superstore when Jared got mad because I wouldn't buy him a truck that he wanted. He had already picked out a movie so I said, "No, you already have a video." Right in the middle of the store he had a huge tantrum and threw the video out of the cart. I said, quietly but firmly, "Now you have nothing." Con sider that, I am a hardened schoolteacher with 20 years' experience. He went absolutely ballistic. Picture this: I'd worked all day, picked up the kids from daycare, shopped for an hour and I had a cart full of items. I was wearing dress shoes, so my feet were killing me, and I was not going to leave—I was going to buy those groceries.

Mustering every ounce of patience in my body I stood in line, with Jared continuing to scream. People were even coming out of the aisles to see what was going on because it sounded like someone was being murdered. I waited patiently, humming to myself. Up walks this lady with a big purple balloon and she asks, "Um, excuse me. May I give him this balloon?" I said, "No, you may certainly not because I am not going to reward his behavior." I proceeded to check out my items and then I took the food to the car with Jared still screaming. I put him into the car seat very calmly then put all the groceries in the trunk. A man who was behind me in the store's checkout line passed by and said, "Is he still screaming?" and I said, "Yes he is." I promptly got in the car and turned the radio up so loud I couldn't hear his screaming. He cried for almost the entire ride home, stopping about a minute before we reached the door. I put him in the house, called my dad and tearfully told him the whole story. Then I asked him, "Did I ever do this to you? Is this normal?" and he said, "No."

By the time I finally took Jared to be tested his language had degenerated into gibberish. I could tell what he was saying, but no one else could understand a word he said. His speech had regressed extensively but I didn't even notice until someone pointed it out. Last summer he was diagnosed at the University of Washington's Autism Center. Prior to that, our other doctors told me that he had Sensory Modulation Disorder and Disruptive Behavior Disorder. Now after all the therapy he's been through Jared talks quite articulately. Linguistically the pragmatics are still confused, but at least everyone can understand the words he's using, even if he isn't using them correctly.

Perhaps this is going to sound odd, but I never expected Jared to be autistic. I was a special education major in college and had seen many children with language delays, but I never saw the diagnosis coming for him. We all knew something was different in his development, though. I remember once, after a particularly intense episode, Jared came to me and said in a little voice, "There's something wrong with me." As many parents have probably done, I let an "expert" talk me out of my concerns. I'd tell the pediatrician about my concerns and she'd say, "Well, do you want him to be autistic?"

To this day, Jared has problems with aggressiveness and hyperactivity, but most of the time he is affectionate and loving. I took Jared to Anchorage with me a month ago and my husband Ray drove us to the airport. Jared's brother Dylan was in the back seat. We got the suitcases out and Dylan was still in his car seat. Jared turned around, went up to his window, knocked, and blew Dylan a kiss. He has come a long way.

Janis's tips

- Learn as much as you can about autism, but don't necessarily make it your whole life. Balance is important. Don't stay with your child 100 percent of the day. Do something for yourself each day. Get a part-time job just to put make-up on and get out of the house. You need a break from kids that are autistic because they are so draining, both physically and emotionally.

- Start a network. Find a role model/mentor to guide you.

- Get as much early intervention as possible; speech, occupational therapy and sensory integration lay the foundations for later development.

- Be an advocate—be strong and speak up for your child's own special needs. Remember, you are the "expert" on your child.

☙

Jean and Jimmy (16)

I am the proud mom of three boys: John, Jimmy, and Jeffery. Jimmy is my middle child and has high-functioning autism, often referred to as Asperger's Syndrome. Jimmy is a sweet kid who enjoys playing video games, and watching movies and *The X Files* on television. He also enjoys any programs, books or videos that he can find related to the weird or occult. Presently, Jimmy's goal is to spend the night at the Lemp Mansion here in St. Louis, which is rumored to be haunted. He also likes to spend time out in the humongous tree house he has built in our backyard. He can work wonders with wood and we often give him more wood as a reward for good behavior. He also enjoys exploring the forest surrounding our neighborhood by himself and making up games in his head. He doesn't have any friends currently.

I first knew something was wrong with Jimmy when he was a few days old. He would not sleep in his crib or the bassinette, instead preferring to sleep in his car seat. When covered with a baby blanket Jimmy would kick it off whether he was awake or asleep. Naps were seldom, leaving me exhausted and afraid. Many times I thought to myself, "Why does this baby cry so much and sleep so little?"

When Jimmy was nine months old, I told the doctor that he didn't play peek-a-boo and that he cried almost all day and most of the night. I also reported that Jimmy wasn't vocalizing the same way his brother had at the same age. The doctor didn't seem the least bit concerned. He thought Jimmy was on track developmentally, although his muscles were a bit underdeveloped. He told me to quit worrying, and hinted that I was just being neurotic because I was pregnant again.

At 15 months, Jimmy had a febrile seizure. He was being treated for a severe sinus infection that appeared to be resistant to antibiotics. It was Sunday afternoon and I was on the phone with my mom and Jimmy was in his crib, taking one of his few naps. My husband had just come home from buying a newspaper and was checking on Jimmy. He yelled to me, "Hon, something's wrong with the baby, he's shaking!" I dropped the phone and ran to the nursery in time to see Jimmy having a seizure. He was burning up with fever. The ordeal lasted for more than five minutes.

On the way to the hospital, Jimmy had several more seizures in my arms. I was terrified; my husband drove as fast as he dared. When we arrived, the emergency room team immediately started an IV and gave Jimmy massive doses of phenobarbital, but Jimmy just wouldn't stop having seizures. He was admitted to the hospital overnight. By the next day the seizures had stopped and the pediatrician sent us home so we could keep an appointment with a well-known ENT (Ear Nose Throat) doctor to treat Jimmy's sinus problem. Between appointments, I brought Jimmy home so I could change his clothes. While standing next to the front door, he fell face forward onto the ground. My little boy had so much medication in his body he couldn't even stand.

Things got worse. After Jimmy had that initial seizure he stopped talking and communicating like before. He could still regularly use a few words that we understood, like "duck," "light," and "uh oh," but it seemed like every time I was able to get him to sleep he would have another seizure and forget whatever additional words he had learned that day. His tantrums began to increase in frequency as well. Jimmy started head banging, throwing himself to the floor with rage, kicking, screaming, arching his back, and pushing away whenever anyone tried to pick him up. He did feed himself but used his fists to scoop the food from his bowl and into his mouth. If the food he was eating was the wrong temperature or texture, he would throw it against the wall. He was so defiant it was overwhelming.

I took Jimmy to two more pediatricians trying to figure out what was wrong. The first of these patted my hand and told me everything would be all right, I should just let Jimmy mature a little. The second met with my husband and me on a Saturday morning. She listened to us but was puzzled by what she heard. Nothing we told her seemed to point to a specific problem. She was confused about the lack of language, the gaining and losing of language skills, and the tantrums. Rather than shooing us out of her office, she had copies of Jimmy's charts sent to her from all the doctors who had treated him. Even with the additional information she informed us Jimmy still did not fit any category of disability. In the end she too patted my hand and said, "Let's wait and see." Wait, wait, wait. That seemed to be every professional's answer and we were no further ahead than before.

When Jimmy was two, I took him to Cardinal Glennon Children's Hospital, a clinic in St. Louis that performs developmental evaluations. Staff at this clinic promised us they would look at all aspects of Jimmy's development: fine motor, gross motor, language skills, and adaptive behavior. Once again we were told what we already knew: Jimmy didn't fit any particular category of disability. The recommendation was to take him home and put him in a good developmental preschool.

At age three Jimmy was still not speaking in sentences. He began receiving speech therapy, five days a week, one hour a day. I would sit in the waiting room playing with baby Jeffery, Jimmy's brother, while listening to Jimmy scream and throw himself against the wall. It took several weeks before he would even let the therapist come near him. The speech pathologist suggested we have him evaluated by an occupational therapist, which we did. It was determined that Jimmy would get an hour of occupational therapy each day in addition to speech therapy.

During these evaluations we were told Jimmy was too high functioning to have autism, despite the fact that he rarely talked, didn't make good eye contact, and had so many sensory issues. However, when Jimmy was six, I asked his neurologist, "Is my son autistic?" He put down his pen and said,

"I've been meaning to talk to you about that." He referred us to a child psychologist at Cardinal Glennon who would be able to give Jimmy that diagnosis provided he fit the criteria. After the psychologist met Jimmy and evaluated him, we were given the diagnosis of Asperger's Syndrome, which at that time was still fairly uncommon. I was so relieved to have some answers and to know that we were not bad parents. At last, I had a name for what was wrong with our son. From that point on, I read and learned everything I could about the disorder so I could help our son to the best of my ability.

Jean's tips

- Always be persistent when dealing with professionals. Don't let the doctors tell you something you know is wrong.

- Get early intervention for your child, either through children's social services or the school.

- Stand your ground with the schools, but remember to be tactful and kind.

- Read, read, and read some more!

- Don't believe everything you read on the Internet, especially the stuff that blames you as a parent for your child's condition. It's not your fault, it never was, and it never will be.

- Accept your child for who he is, not what you dreamed he would be. You'll both be happier in the long run.

ᏇᎡ

Jenny and Liam (6)

Liam is funny, mischievous, naughty, sweet, cuddly, defiant, active, and good at using a shy smile and the word "please" to get what he wants. He loves to jump in puddles, throw rocks in the water, and drive snowmobiles and jet skis as fast as he can (or should I say as fast as the driver will take him). In many other ways, though, Liam is very different from his typical peers.

Some things come easier for Liam than for other kids. He taught himself to read when he was four and although he has not even started kindergarten, he reads like a second grader. He has navigated a computer, the Internet and cable TV menus for years without anyone teaching him how. He has an amazing capacity for numbers and can count to 100 by ones, fives and tens. What is particularly amazing to me is how he remembers numbers. For example, he likes tracks 3 and 8 on one CD and 5, 16 and 24 on another—he asks for songs by track number on any CD we put in. He can also act out every Disney movie or Nick Jr. show imaginable, including the previews.

Unfortunately, there are many more things that are harder for Liam than they are for other kids. Liam has trouble understanding spoken language. This causes him a lot of frustration because he doesn't always know what is going on. He can't understand where we are going and for how long, how to do something and what the rules are, when we tell him. Liam also doesn't really know how to play with toys or other kids, so he doesn't have any friends. He likes to be with people, but doesn't know how to do the same things as them—or isn't interested in the same things. Liam has trouble concentrating on things that people ask him to do. He reserves all of his focus and concentration for the things that interest him. That makes it hard for him to learn to do other things. Liam has lots of movies stored in his head, so he can readily play them back if he isn't engaged in whatever is happening in the present. Liam also perseverates on things—he can't get a movie or scene or phrase from a game out of his head.

Liam started changing at about 20 months old. He stopped noticing Dad come home from work and stopped using words he had commonly used. Whereas he had been easy-going as an infant, he started getting upset easily. We attributed this regression to post-traumatic stress because Liam was badly burned in a fire when he was 19 months old. Neither his doctor nor any family members thought anything of these changes other than that they were a reaction to being burned.

When Liam was 26 months, he began attending a Montessori school. Each day the teacher shared her insights into his irregular behavior, but it didn't connect with me that there was something seriously wrong. About a month after starting school, we went away for a weekend with some friends and Liam's behavior became completely unmanageable. He spent hours banging his head on the wall and having tantrums. On Monday, I asked the aide in his room if she thought Liam's behaviour was normal. The aide responded, "If it was my son, I'd get him evaluated." I spoke with the head teacher later that day and she told me how to explain to my doctor what was occurring. Up until then I had never been able to verbalize what the problem was. She explained that kids his age are egocentric, but Liam was overly so. She also said that he didn't play like the other kids.

The very next day, I went to see our pediatrician and told him what the teacher had said about Liam. The doctor asked if I thought he was autistic and I said, "I don't know, maybe," knowing nothing about autism. I went home and searched the web. From reading the descriptions, it seemed like autism was a reasonable possibility. I called an acquaintance who had a son with autism and talked to her later that day. She directed me to a store, the Autism Resource Network, and I was able to talk to the owner and get some books.

The first book I picked up, *Facing Autism* (by L.M. Hamilton, 2000), described Liam perfectly. That evening I told my family and friends about my suspicions. My husband and our friends were on board right away, realizing that it was highly likely that Liam did indeed have autism. Both my parents and my mother-in-law started doing their own research too and they agreed with our conclusions.

I believe the first time I heard the word autism in reference to my son was in 2001 when he was 27 months old. By the time we had the second appointment we were convinced that Liam had autism and that it was in his best interest to get autism rather than PDD-NOS or anything else as his diagnosis. We told the psychologists right up front what we anticipated and how we felt about the diagnosis. A month later, Liam was officially diagnosed with autism.

Liam's diagnosis was from Fraser, an organization recognized for diagnosis of autism. It has a day treatment program for communication and interaction disorders, an inclusive preschool program, as well as a new inclusion grade school with 50 percent of the students having special needs. Liam began going to special education preschool in December and entered the day treatment program in January.

I'm happy to say that I don't fear for Liam's future—I have hope. I hope Liam will feel happy and that he is contributing. For him, I think that will mean having a job where he uses his intelligence, but at this point it doesn't matter what it is. Right now it is difficult to say what Liam will achieve. I would wager it is equally probable that he will collect shopping carts at the grocery store as it is that he will get a Ph.D. in physics. I'm aiming for something in the middle and fighting for him to have every chance at that Ph.D.

Jenny's tips

- Remember, we are in this together. There are so many parents who are willing to help each other out; share stories, share resources, and be one another's emotional support. You aren't alone.

- Find friends within the community with whom you can share your experiences.

CR

Karen and Dylan (7)

Dylan is a pretty happy kid as long as I don't alter his routine. Overall he lives in his own little world, and his world is perfect. He amuses himself by going from cartoon to computer to PlayStation and back to the computer. He has few self-help skills and needs something different from me every five seconds. His expressive language is about two years delayed and his receptive language is at a six-year-old's level. He's not verbal in your typical six-year-old sense, though. He doesn't tell you when he's hungry, tired, or not feeling well. Most of his verbal skills are echolalia. For instance, he repeats things he's heard on the TV or radio, or seen on a video. When other people are around they say, "Oh, you really don't have conversations with him." They are right in some respects, but we still communicate.

I knew when I brought Dylan home from the hospital that something was wrong. Everybody else thought I was just a thirtysomething mom. We have another child who is 15 now and every time I'd make an observation about something odd that Dylan did I got a response like, "Well, you haven't had a child in eight years; this is relatively new again to you. You've forgotten everything; you're like a new mom all over." Still I knew something was wrong. He was content to lie in his crib for hours and hours. I would pick him up and he'd stiffen like he didn't want me to touch him. When I'd talk he wouldn't follow my voice; he would stare straight ahead. He would sit in his swing for hours if we let him. Everybody kept saying, "He's an easy baby. He is so good; don't go looking for problems."

At a year old the rage and self-injury started, and all of a sudden everybody was saying, "Oh, something is not right." Dylan was four before we found the right doctor to help him. It wasn't a pediatrician; it was actually a medical doctor here in town that made the initial diagnosis. The doctor's mother ran a school for developmentally disabled children. She had started the school so the doctor had attended with his mother when he was little. He was able to recognize the symptoms. Even so, he wouldn't guarantee his own judgment, and he sent us to Children's Hospital to get more extensive testing done.

When I left the doctor's office the day we received the diagnosis, I bawled my eyes out. Yet I was also relieved at the same time because Dylan was out of control and we finally knew what was wrong. He couldn't tell us his wants and needs and I was constantly blaming myself for his problems. With someone telling me it wasn't my fault I felt better, but at the same time I was heartbroken.

Ironically, when Dylan received the diagnosis, I had been reading about autism. I have a sister-in-law who is a speech pathologist and she works with autistic children in Minnesota. One day I called her and described over the phone what was happening and she said, "Have you ever heard of autism?" and I said, "Yes, I've heard of it, but I don't really know what it is." Her reply was simply, "You need to do some research." I looked autism up on the Internet and found a lot of the characteristic behaviors that resembled Dylan's, so it didn't come as a complete shock to me that was what he had. It wasn't until he actually received the diagnosis I started reading everything I could get my hands on.

The most fearful thing about autism is the unknown. You don't know what your child is going to grow up and be like. That is the worst part—not knowing. Most of the time when a child has a disorder or illness, you can predict fairly well what the outcome will be, and you know what their lives are going to be like and the obstacles they face. With autism there are so many factors that determine how your child will end up. You may find a treatment that works. You may try several different interventions and therapies with varying degrees of success. All you can do is hope for the best.

Karen's tips

- Talk about it. If you don't, you'll explode!

- Remember, you may be tough and strong, but you don't have to go through this alone.

- The sooner you accept the diagnosis, the sooner you can get on with helping your child.

- There are so many options and perspectives out there—you have to find what works for your child.

CR

Kelli and Aidan (2)

Even though at 18 months my son Aidan was still not very verbal, I figured all that would change when he started Mother's Day Out (part time child care programs designed to give stay-home moms a break from their daily routine). Fairly soon after he began the program, I began getting reports on my son's odd behavior. During assembly all the children would gather in a large circle. Often, Aidan would run out in the middle of the circle and dance. At first, the teachers were amused, but as he continually disrupted assembly I could sense that he was becoming a problem child.

From my work as a nurse, I knew some things about age-appropriate behavior and development for children. One fact that stood out in my mind was that children typically behave better at school than at home. Aidan was completely the opposite. As the negative reports from the Mother's Day Out program continued to arrive, I decided to consult a pediatrician. The doctor went through a battery of questions and nothing seemed too out of the ordinary. Then the doctor called Aidan's name and he wouldn't look. Three times he called Aidan's name and still no response (red flag). Then he asked another question that made me nervous, "Does he ever make eye contact?" (red flag number two). After administering some easy developmental tasks, the doctor informed me that he thought Aidan had PDD, a form of autism. He referred us to Early Intervention.

Soon after the tentative diagnosis by the pediatrician, a team from Early Intervention evaluated Aidan. The speech therapist indicated that Aidan had both expressive and receptive language delays. The physical therapist also found delays, although Aidan's gross motor skills were good. The physical therapist hypothesized that many of the physical delays may have been inaccurate due to the fact that Aidan couldn't follow the directions the therapist was giving him. When I asked if he was autistic, they said, "No" as a group.

My husband Stephen and I were relieved. Although we didn't know a great deal about autism yet, we knew enough that we didn't want Aidan to have it. Then one day I happened to turn on the news and there was a five-part special about autism on that week. I *never* watch the news so it felt like I was meant to turn on the TV that day. On the second day, the boy in the program was exactly like Aidan. He was laughing and smiling but doing his own thing in his own little world. I felt my heart in my stomach. That night I made my husband watch it and at that point there was no doubt in our minds.

The next day we called Early Intervention to get Aidan re-evaluated. We were told that we would need to wait six months before the next evaluation. My husband became irate and said something to the effect of, "So it's our fault you didn't tell us our son had autism?" At that point the person on the other end of the line became apologetic. The director of the program had no idea that autism was even a speculation in this case. In fact, no one on the diagnostic team that visited our home and evaluated Aidan was capable of making that diagnosis in the first place. A behaviorist was sent to re-evaluate the situation and Aidan was formally diagnosed.

I used to work weekends so that I could have weekdays free to enjoy, but now it's all about Aidan. Our preoccupation with Aidan's challenges has been very stressful on my relationship with my husband. In the past seven years that we've been married we've seldom fought about anything. We never went to bed mad. Now sometimes we won't speak for two or three days because of the stress.

For now, I try to hold the pieces of my life together. If I didn't do so hot one day, I try to start fresh the next day. I know that the blood, sweat, and tears we put in to helping Aidan will continue indefinitely. The very thought of it is overwhelming, but I also know that the day we stop trying is the day he will stop responding. The price he would pay is too high to consider. I try to remember that this is out of our control. Although we have control over the choices we make and the avenues of therapy we explore, our higher power is ultimately the one who is in control, knows the plan, and can see the bigger picture. I have to have faith that we aren't supposed to see the bigger picture just yet—only day by day.

Kelli's tip

- See each day as a new beginning.

CR

Kelly and Shaelyn (4)

"Please stand up dear, please…please?" I pleaded again and again. "Mommy just wants you to go outside the theater and into the mall. We can go in the balloon pit." I use diversion at least 15 times a day and hoped it would work this time too. "You have done so well through the whole movie, why are you melting down now?" The more I talked the more out of control my daughter became. She was melting again, but this time in front of hundreds of people. I pleaded, I begged, I bargained, but the more I spoke the more violently she threw her little body all over the place. With despair and nothing else to do, I picked my Shaelyn up over my shoulder and carried her out of the theater.

As eyes glared at me, I wanted to scream, "What are you looking at? Don't you understand something is seriously wrong with my daughter? She can't help it; I can't help it, just go on with your day and ignore us. She isn't bad and I am not a bad mother, so please, go away!" As my frustration grew, I heard security being called. Frozen to the spot, I knew it wouldn't be long before I melted down too.

"Ma'am, can you hold on, please?" the uniformed guard said to me as he looked down at my out-of-control daughter, and then to Shaelyn,

"Sweetie, is this your mother?" She sat there yelling and uncontrollably sobbing without looking at a single soul. If only she had a sticker on her back or forehead that said "I have a developmental disorder" things would be so much easier. I explained, "My daughter is in fact my daughter, sir. Please look at my driver's license; look at all the pictures of my children in my wallet." To my relief, he was satisfied.

As the crowd stared on, I thanked the guard for letting us go. I picked my daughter up and carried her over my shoulder because she was still melting down at that point and I knew she wouldn't walk willingly on her own. By the time I got to the car and got my daughter into the car seat she was sobbing, but calmer. I got into the driver's seat without starting the car and started sobbing heavily myself. I looked at my beautiful girl in the back seat, took her hand and just held it. There was nothing I could do to soothe her. Within five minutes, she dozed off to sleep, exhausted by the day's adventure. I cried the whole way home. When I arrived, my husband saw my puffy, swollen eyes as I parked the car, and immediately took over. I isolated myself in the bedroom where I could collect myself and reflect on the day's events.

On June, 6 2001 Children and Youth services had called me at work and said, "We have a little girl here, just three months old," and asked if we would take her. We had been foster parents for a few years but previously always had boys; so I was delighted when I found out we'd have a little girl this time. My husband just happened to be home that day from work. I called him at home ecstatic with the news. Having three almost grown children already, his response was, "Darling, do you really want to start over with an infant?" I ordered, "Meet me on the highway in a half an hour with a car seat, and please, since you are home today, put the crib back up."

I left work and made the long drive to the agency. They took me to a small room and my heart skipped a beat. She had no hair, but the most piercing blue eyes I ever saw. She also had a big dimple on her chin, which is my weakness. When we got home, reactions were mixed. Our little girl was the crankiest thing, and my husband was scared to hold her at first because she was so small. We found out that she had been in foster care the preceding night, but the family could not take the colic and returned her to the agency the next morning. The colic lasted for some time, but I didn't notice anything too out of the ordinary.

A month later, I got a call from the agency asking, if need be, would we be interested in adopting the little girl? If not, they would have to take her and place her in a pre-adoptive house. I knew in my heart that I wanted to keep her, but I could not make the decision alone. This matter was for the whole family, and everyone would be a part of the decision. After all, our lives would be changed forever by the decision. The older children were supportive and my husband said explicitly, "This is my baby girl and she will go nowhere else. Here is where she belongs." She would be ours forever if necessary.

On November 4, 2002 Shaelyn became our legal adoptive daughter and it was one of the happiest days of our lives. She was 18 months old. She had some delays developmentally, but it didn't matter. By then we loved her so much we couldn't imagine life without her. Family members, friends, and employers were all supportive of the adoption. Our co-workers even threw baby showers for us. We received cards and gifts in the mail; it was a joyous occasion.

However, our joy was marred with apprehension. At two years old, we had concerns about Shaelyn's speech. She seemed to say some things earlier on, but word progression was at a halt. Most of the time she babbled like a baby, and I could not understand anything she said. We hardly ever knew what she wanted. At daycare, she was aggressive and bit other children. She had trouble eating, and would often choke on foods or swallow things whole. She would spit out certain foods and cry if exposed to certain textures.

Other sensory issues were noticeable as well. Shaelyn put every single thing into her mouth and drooled like a baby. She also ate paper, cardboard, dirt, rocks, and had no regard for rules or safety. She was always on the go and even chose not to sleep half the time. We first noticed hand flapping while she was engaged in watching her favorite television program, *Sesame Street*. She was constantly moving and shifting her feet, which we now know indicates sensory overload. I called for an IEP meeting to have her evaluated again and they determined Shaelyn had moderate dysphasia thereby qualifying to receive physical therapy and intense speech therapy.

Through all of this, my pediatrician assured me Shaelyn would catch up and things would indeed be normal. When she was three and a half years old I sought help from another pediatrician, who referred us to a neurologist. Like most parents, we were dumbfounded when the neurologist asked my husband and me if we had ever considered she might be autistic. "Autistic," I thought, "Wasn't that the thing where kids do nothing all day except just sit and flap their hands and flip cards? This can't be true, she doesn't do that and she knows her ABCs. She can count and knows her colors. Heck, she can even count in Spanish. She does have some minor obsession, but she is young, right? Won't she grow out of it? She even has some eye contact and hugs me all the time."

Apparently the evidence was there all along for those who knew what they were looking for. For example, Shaelyn climbed on us constantly, as well as on every single thing in her bedroom. At the time we didn't realize it, but as the neurologist put it, "she treated us like furniture." She was cruel to animals and often hurt people without realizing it. We thought she was just rough. Looking back we recognize all the bruises she was constantly getting were a result of non-stop movement combined with a higher threshold for pain.

The neurologist gave us information on Asperger's Syndrome and prescribed Risperdal to resolve sleeping issues. This medication stopped Shaelyn's wrist turning and she is now sleeping at least seven hours a night. Her behavior is much more tolerable than before. Don't get me wrong, it's hardly a cure, but there has been much improvement. With increased sleep, she started speaking a little better and functioning without constant agitation.

After all the hypothesizing about autism and Asperger's Syndrome, the tentative diagnosis has changed. Another professional recently labeled Shaelyn's problems as Neurologically Impaired. I have faith in his expertise. At her most recent IEP meeting, it was also suggested that she has Sensory Integration Dysfunction and I have requested yet another evaluation. So, for now, the grand total is Neurologically Impaired with expressive speech delay, fine and gross motor delays, Sensory Integration Dysfunction, and ADHD. I wonder if the diagnosis will change again or can we just stop here? She still eats non-food items, but I feel that may be related to sensory problems, rather than true pica. Educationally, she falls under the diagnosis of PDD-NOS, but with a diagnosis of Neurological Impairment she qualifies for inclusion in a separate program. Everything is so confusing, especially when so many potential diagnoses have been suggested.

I don't blame anyone for the long wait for a diagnosis; I simply use this to motivate me to help others press for a faster one. Children are frequently misdiagnosed (see "A professional's perspective" at the end of this chapter). They are often found to have ADHD, which happened to us, or told they will grow out of it. Now it is evident that Shaelyn will not "grow out of it," so we just have to take the label at face value and move on.

Today Shaelyn is four years old, her speech is taking off, and she is a pleasure to be around. She still gets occupational therapy, speech therapy, and is in a specialized preschool. I would walk on water and back for her. She did not choose to be on this earth, but it is up to us to make sure earth and life are the best possible places for her to be. Shaelyn is our princess and we love her just as dearly as any other member of the family.

Unfortunately, people still ask me if we regret getting ourselves into all this, meaning would we adopt her again knowing what we know now. The answer is: absolutely. She is our pride and joy and we love her as if she came straight from my womb. Her diagnosis does not change the happiness she has brought to our lives. Thinking of all the wonderful funny things she does or says every single day warms my heart.

We thank God every day for our little girl. I thank Him for choosing us to be Shaelyn's parents. Yes, it is hard sometimes. Sure, we can't do many outings or go out to eat every night, but so what? Whenever I look at her smile, I know it is all worth it. Life will go on, people will learn, resources will become more readily available; we will be here for our daughter, no matter what. She is a gift and we plan on treasuring our gift forever, perfect or not.

Kelly's tips

- Always remember that you are doing your best.

- Remember, no one can possibly understand your life until they have walked a mile in your shoes.

- You are special because you have dealt with the issue at hand and still are dealing with it.

- You are not alone.

ℭℛ

Susan and Mark (10)

Mark currently attends year-round school. He likes watching videos and has also recently taken up Nintendo DS. He loves anything dangerous or high speed. Climbing trees and long bike rides with his dad are among his preferred activities.

Mark must exit the same door he entered and has to have two of everything. He has poor fine motor activity, but excellent gross motor skills. He perseverates on favorite subjects like bridges in different cities, states, and countries. He often requests that we sing him songs to the tune of "Take me out to the ballgame"—for example, "Take me out to Target, buy me a new video." He loves bridges and has become a good traveler so we have begun planning family vacations around interesting bridges.

At birth Mark had atypical strabismus, so he has been under the watchful eye of a neurologist and other specialists since the age of three months.

The neurologist was the first to ever tell us that our child had "developmental delays." Our pediatrician was angry about the observation and was surprised that we would continue follow-up with the neurologist. We enrolled Mark in Early Intervention, speech therapy, and occupational therapy.

After seeing other specialists, we decided to go along with the theory that everything was okay. They reassured us that he was just a boy and his sister did all the talking for him. However, he had some issues that we couldn't ignore such as delayed speech, low motor tone, and other peculiarities. Mark would have a fit whenever someone came into our home, and went through a period where all the lights had to be on. He also chewed his clothing. In daycare at age two, he'd sit in the corner and flip through books all day while the other children played. The final straw that made me realize that something was not right about my child was the day we stopped for donuts on the way to daycare. In order for the kids to have time to eat the donuts, I drove around a bit. Mark absolutely freaked about the change in routine and deviation from our normal route.

For many years we continued to follow up with the neurologist who had been the first to say something was different with our child. Through her notes, we can trace how Mark's autism actually blossomed. In retrospect, I think the Early Intervention team, and the speech and occupational therapists were trying to tell us they thought he was autistic but we weren't listening to them. I had been reassured for so long that everything would be okay I naively believed "developmental delayed" simply meant that things were just delayed. I had never even heard of PDD.

The Maryland Infants and Toddlers program was the first to actually diagnose Mark as autistic and mentally retarded. I had never felt my heart sink before, but it did that day, even though I had no idea what it all meant. The Internet was still in its early stages, but even then I found quite a bit of information on autism. I read the autism checklist and nodded "maybe" as I read down the list of criteria. Even with the data staring me in the face it was still difficult to accept. The most current statistic I found said that autism occurred in 1 in 10,000 children at that time.

Following the diagnosis we received a series of educational recommendations that included moving to Delaware and enrolling Mark in the Delaware Autism Program. That was one of the best decisions I've made in my life! The program has made a tremendous difference for all of us.

After living with autism for seven years now, I hardly remember a time without it. Autism is part of every minute of every day. We definitely have to plan activities, meals and vacations around Mark, but things have gotten better over the years and now we can travel, go to restaurants, and leave him "unattended" for periods of time. Our lives demand careful scheduling and routine but, with the proper reinforcers in place, we go places like the grocery store, the barber, the doctor's office, and on vacations without a problem; we even take different routes to get there! Mark is a sweet, affectionate, happy kid, who is an endless source of amusement.

Susan's tip

- Learn to work with it!

CR

Theresa and Josiah (7)

My son Josiah is the second of three children born to me and my husband. I also have a stepson, Jon, who has been in my life since he was two, so I consider him my child as well. My husband and I experienced five years of infertility and at one point were told we would never have children.

Josiah was different from birth. I remember overhearing the nurses talking about him during a shift change—he was very demanding. Several months passed before I could get him to sleep anywhere other than on my body. He nursed voraciously, giving me blood blisters on my nipples on four separate occasions due to the intensity of his sucking. He cried any time he could not visibly see me, and his level of attachment and neediness seemed to intensify as he grew. As an infant he essentially lived in his sling and as a toddler I carried him in the baby backpack until he became too heavy.

For three weeks after receiving his six-month inoculations Josiah had seizures. His sleep became much more disturbed, and he began biting and pulling my hair. He would bite 50 to 80 times per day, leaving bruises all over my body. He would pull my hair until my scalp was sore, and would weep hysterically if he was not in physical contact with my body.

I talked to his doctor, who told me to ignore Josiah's behavior and recommended books on helping your baby sleep, implying that Josiah's difficulties were the result of my parenting skills. He told me that there were no services available for my child until he reached age three. Finally, when Josiah bit my niece to the point of drawing blood, I got angry with the pediatrician and demanded that Josiah be evaluated. If my parenting was to blame, I needed someone to look at Josiah and then teach me how to parent him. Ultimately, I received help when we went in for a sick visit and saw a nurse practitioner who made the referral for us.

We took Josiah to a full-day developmental clinic at Mid Maine Medical Center where seven different specialists saw him in one day. Although their diagnosis was not the ultimate one, it helped to get the ball rolling. Within two months we had occupational therapy, speech therapy, and physical therapy in place for Josiah. When Josiah was first evaluated, in December 1999, he received a generic diagnosis of Regulatory Disorder. At a follow-up examination three months later the diagnosis of PDD was proposed, but I did not want him labeled. Josiah was formally diagnosed with autism more than two years later, at which point the label was necessary for him to receive certain educational services. He carries the additional diagnosis of Early Onset Bipolar Disorder.

In one way I was relieved by the diagnosis because I could see Josiah's behavior in a new light. For years I had tried just about every suggestion that well-meaning friends and family gave me, but all had failed. My emotions fluctuated between guilt and self-condemnation about my capability as a parent, and I also felt anger and frustration with Josiah at how he was disrupting our lives. The other part of me truly grieved because of the challenges I knew lay ahead for him.

My life has changed in so many ways since Josiah's diagnosis it is difficult to express in words. Perhaps the easiest way to sum it up is to say that my world has been dramatically reduced in size. In reality, many of the things that I no longer have time for in my life were actually things that were keeping me from growing. Prior to having Josiah, I had prayed to God not to give me a mentally handicapped child because I feared I could not handle it. With Josiah I have learned that I have a gift for working with these special children.

Theresa's tips

- Seek out every victory in your child's life, no matter how small, and celebrate it.

- Stay focused on today. Trying to predict how your child will be in the future can be so overwhelming it becomes difficult to enjoy the present.

- Trust your instincts. No one knows your child like you do.

- Take care of yourself and take time for yourself.

CR

A professional's perspective: Dan Ingram, Certified School Psychologist

Over a 33-year career as a developmental psychologist, I have had the opportunity to observe, assess, and treat a wide variety of children and families from preschool through young adulthood. For the past 13 years I have specialized in working with children and families who are dealing with the many challenges of Autism Spectrum Disorder.

Gaining the needed expertise to help children with Autism Spectrum Disorder and their families has required many years of additional study, research, and work. I am particularly interested in assessment and diagnosis. I feel very strongly that a successful treatment program begins with an accurate and comprehensive assessment. As professionals we are ethically obligated to provide parents with the best possible assessment and interventions. To meet this challenge, professionals must continually educate themselves in all aspects of Autism Spectrum Disorder. Many professionals choose to specialize in a specific disorder as a result of a family connection, or due to a special child or family with whom they have worked. In my case one specific young lady who was destined to be labeled Behaviorally Disordered and placed in a class for socially–emotionally disordered children was the child who launched my interest in Autism Spectrum Disorder. In her case I was convinced that the disorder was the primary disability and she required specialized treatment and intervention. Thus began my interest and focus on children and families living and dealing with Autism Spectrum Disorder.

Pervasive Developmental Disorders are a very complex group of disorders. There are three distinct disorders that fall under this category related to Autism Spectrum Disorder. First and foremost is autism. The *Diagnostic and Statistical Manual–Fourth Edition–Test Revision* (DSM–IV–TR) identifies a number of specific criteria that must be met in order to make a diagnosis of autism. Broadly speaking, these fall into three categories:

- social interaction

- communication

- behaviors, interests, and activities.

Unless specific criteria within these three categories are met, a diagnosis of autism cannot be made. A diagnosis of Asperger's Disorder, which is very similar to autism in many respects, has to meet distinctly different criteria in

order to make a diagnosis. When diagnosing Asperger's Disorder professionals use criteria that fall within the following two broad categories:

* social interaction
* behaviors, interests, and activities.

While these are the same categories from which specific criteria are
required for a diagnosis of autism, it is important to note that there must be
no delays in the following two areas of development:

* language
* cognitive ability.

The latter assumes at least average intellectual potential. These two important areas are what separate the two disorders.

The remaining diagnosis is Pervasive Developmental Disorder-Not
Otherwise Specified (PDD-NOS). PDD-NOS is an exclusionary diagnosis
and essentially states that, if the child does not meet the criteria for autism
or Asperger's Disorder but has atypical behavior patterns, then a diagnosis
of PDD-NOS can be made. This diagnosis is often confusing for parents
and some professionals. The diagnosis of PDD-NOS is sometimes referred
to as "atypical autism."

Obviously, making a differential diagnosis of one of the Pervasive
Developmental Disorders is quite complex and a comprehensive evaluation
should be conducted prior to making a final diagnosis. In my opinion,
a comprehensive evaluation requires observing the child in multiple
environments over multiple occasions (e.g. school, home, community),
interviewing caregivers and parents using standardized checklists (e.g.
Childhood Autism Rating Scale, Autism Diagnostic Interview-Revised,
Asperger's Diagnostic Checklist), and conducting a formal assessment
using a standardized instrument (e.g. Autism Diagnostic Observation
Schedule-Western Psychological Services (WPS)). A comprehensive
assessment as described above provides the most accurate and detailed
information to the professional prior to making a formal diagnosis and
developing a comprehensive treatment program. A comprehensive evaluation by an experienced professional will enable the professional to answer
the many questions that will be asked by the parents when a diagnosis is
made. When a child is diagnosed with autism, Asperger's Disorder, or PDD
presumably there will be a thorough discussion about both the long-term
and short-term implications of the disorder, what services are available to

help the child, and who can deliver the most up-to-date treatment and intervention programs. Unfortunately, not all clinicians provide the same standard of care in this respect.

In some instances there are disagreements between professionals over a diagnosis. When this occurs the parents are placed in a difficult situation and can feel pulled in different directions. If a disagreement occurs there are several options for the parents. There is always the possibility of a third opinion, which may resolve the situation or may add even more confusion. My suggestion would be to assess the quality and comprehensiveness of the diagnostic assessment and the expertise and experience of the professionals conducting the evaluation. Parents should be aware that titles and advanced academic credentials do not always ensure competency. When seeking an evaluation parents should "do their homework," ask pertinent questions of the professional relating to their experience and training, and find out whether the evaluation will be comprehensive prior to agreeing to an assessment. Parents should also be aware there are other disorders (e.g. Social Phobia, Obsessive-Compulsive Disorder, Language Processing Disorders) that can present behaviors similar to autism and Asperger's Disorder. The professional conducting the assessment must rule out these and other disorders prior to making a final formal diagnosis of autism or Asperger's Disorder.

Similarly, parents should trust their instincts relative to the need for their child to have a formal assessment. Many times parents are encouraged to wait by professionals when they innately feel something is deviant in their child's developmental patterns. When in doubt it is best to pursue an assessment from a competent professional. Pervasive Developmental Disorders research literature clearly supports the supposition that early diagnosis and intensive treatment provide the best long-term outcome.

A final point of inquiry often made by parents is regarding the severity of the disorder. Many parents want and need to know, "Does my child fall within the mild, moderate, or severe range of autism or Asperger's?" While this is a straightforward and legitimate question from parents the answer is often difficult to pin down. There are so many variables that affect the expression of behaviors associated with Autism Spectrum Disorders, and treatment programs can be very effective in alleviating symptoms, that a qualitative rating such as mild, moderate, or severe is relative and transient. Personally, I do my best to answer the parents as to where their child is presenting at a certain moment in time but assure them that their child will make progress, and the expression of the disorder will fluctuate and change over a period of time.

Once parents receive a diagnosis it is very likely they may experience a grief reaction similar to when a death occurs. The grief response varies tremendously from family to family in terms of severity, intensity, and duration. Parents cannot be "moved through" their grief reaction. It can be as short as a week or as long as several years in duration. In addition, a grief reaction can, and often does, reoccur as the child moves through predictable life stages and life events (e.g. entry into school, dating, proms). Parents would be advised to establish an ongoing relationship with a competent, trusted professional to support and assist them through their journey. Truly, having a child with Autism Spectrum Disorder is a "marathon" not a "sprint," and parents need and deserve all the support they can obtain from competent caring professionals who are up to date in their knowledge, assessment practices, and treatment paradigms.

SOMETHING TO TALK ABOUT

1. How has your life changed since the diagnosis?

2. Where do you see yourself in terms of accepting the diagnosis?

3. What advice would you give to someone who just received a diagnosis for their child?

4. How can you overcome the guilt and anger that often accompany a diagnosis?

5. Share your diagnosis story with a friend or group of friends.

6. What advice would you give to doctors, psychiatrists, and counselors who are involved with giving autism/developmental disability diagnoses? Email your ideas to diagnosisautism@gmail.com.

REFLECTION ACTIVITY

Write "your story" about autism in a journal or diary. Use the questions in Appendix A as a guide.

2.

Therapy, Treatment, and Intervention…Oh My!

Farrah and Mia (6)

Mia starts her day around 6:00 a.m. and goes strong until about 7:00 at night. We are constantly running after her—she gets into everything! Mia has severe pica in addition to autism so she eats practically anything. I have to watch over her 24/7. She was growing normally until she was about six months old and then she stopped developing. By ten months old she was diagnosed as "globally delayed." She wasn't diagnosed with autism and mental retardation until age four so that is when she really started getting help. When I received the diagnosis, I had known something was seriously wrong so my reaction was, "Let's get working. Let's get her going." I was ready to jump into the research and find out what we needed to do. My husband was in denial but I kept telling him, "She's not going to get better unless we help her to get over it—so let's get going!" He had no other choice but to go along with me. I kept saying, "You can't feel sorry for her, you just have to get over it!"

My life is more hectic now than it used to be, there's a lot more to do. It's been therapy, therapy, therapy for so long it seems there is not much time for anything else. Right now we're concentrating our efforts on fundraising to get an autism service dog. The dog would be trained in search and rescue, which would be extremely helpful because if we happen to leave a door open or look away for a minute, Mia's gone! If she did escape, the dog would be able to find her and bring her home. The dogs are taught to assist with a variety of daily tasks as well as providing constant companionship.

Regrettably, the cost for the dog is $12,000 and that doesn't even include the time we would spend in Ohio for training. Training with a new owner takes ten days. Mia would also attend to make sure the dog was a good match for her. We contacted an organization called the Sunshine Foundation to see if they could make her dream come true; Mia loves dogs and seems to have a special bond with them. When she was little we had a dog and she absolutely loved him; in turn it was almost like the dog sensed something was wrong with her. He would constantly guard over her. Due to the severity of her needs, I think an autism service dog would be a perfect match.

Eventually I hope Mia will learn to talk. She does use some words but the speech therapist doesn't think she will ever be able to speak in sentences. I'm not giving up. Mia is so social, everyone keeps telling me she's too involved with other people to be autistic. I say, "No, that's because I work with her and make her sit down and interact and play with me." She hasn't always been like that; I've worked with her day after day.

A lot of parents I've talked to say, "I can't do this, I give up!" They are ready to ship their kids off to a group home or some institution. I can't see me ever doing that to Mia. I can't imagine not having enough hope to keep trying. Each day there is new hope. There are also new challenges as well as new behaviors—when you finally get rid of one there is another. I've learned a lot from Mia—the greatest lesson being, never take life for granted. Other people go on with their busy days and never have to think about anything else. With Mia I have learned to pay more attention to what is important, my children.

Farrah's tips

- Don't judge a book by its cover. If a child is acting out in public, don't automatically assume they have a bad parent, you never know if there's an underlying problem.

- Don't ever accept what the doctors tell you as fact. They say Mia will never talk—I say, "Never say never!"

ᗯ

Jamie and Sarah (6)

Following Sarah's diagnosis I was devastated. In a lot of ways I was glad to get the diagnosis: now that I knew what was wrong I could start getting help. However, my greatest shock came when I realized that there was very little help for Sarah in the part of Tennessee where we live. There were no facilities available, no special schools in the area, and there were no qualified therapists.

After receiving the diagnosis, my next step was to network. I think I called every number there was to call related to autism. I must have made at least a hundred phone calls to different parts of the country. Surprisingly, the most helpful "resource" was talking to other parents. The social worker who initially suspected Sarah had autism gave me the name of some mothers in the area and they provided me with the information I needed. They directed me to county schools rather than city schools, and gave me a specific recommendation on the best curriculum coordinator. I followed their advice and identified adequate services to get started. Another parent helped me contact a branch of the Association for Retarded Citizens (Arc) (Sarah has a dual diagnosis of autism and mental retardation) to try and get additional services and funding for a home therapy program.

Currently, Sarah qualifies for the Medicaid waiver program because her behavior is so severe. Over the years I have filled out tons of paperwork and spent many hours in meetings to obtain services for her. Once a caseworker from the Department of Children's Services came out to help us, but they still cut the number of therapy hours per week. Of course, I fought and got them back. Now, though, I'm faced with a situation where I have enough hours available but I don't have any competent therapists. All the funding in the world doesn't matter if you don't have qualified people to administer the program.

Based on 30 years of research, we chose to use Applied Behavioral Analysis (ABA) with Discreet Trial Training (DTT) as the foundation for our home program. Many children experience dramatic improvements in behavior, language, and social skills through these programs. Sarah's results are mixed. About a year and a half into the program I realized she wasn't going to spontaneously recover. I began to lose hope and I suspected Sarah was never going to be what you would call a "typical" child.

We've also tried biological testing. I sent samples of Sarah's hair, urine, feces, and blood to laboratories to be analyzed. Next I purchased vitamins, but it was practically impossible to get them into her. For a while we tried the gluten-free, casein-free (GFCF) diet but that didn't seem to help either. Sarah ate hardly anything during the entire time we were on the diet and began losing weight. When the GFCF diet failed I thought, "Oh no, that didn't work either. She's going to be like this forever." Again the situation seemed hopeless.

Looking back, it seems silly to have given up because there's always hope. In this case, the Lord's lesson was, "Wait!" I couldn't understand why I was being led to all these innovative therapies that were helping lots of other kids but not mine. Now I see how everything had to occur that way. Lessons had to be learned. I know everything happens for a reason; we don't always see the big picture. Whereas my other children teach me how to be a good mother, Sarah teaches me how to be a good person.

Sometimes I feel frustrated because I am unable to help Sarah. I can't communicate with her and I can't help her break out of this. I know there is somebody in there. Sometimes Sarah will do something or say something that's so normal, but in an instant she's gone. While I know there is somebody in there trying to get out, it is maddening not having the means to know what to do or how to do it.

Naturally, some of the best moments are when we do get through, when Sarah grasps a concept in therapy or when I know I've reached her. We are always working to teach her functional skills and it's wonderful when there's something tangible to show for it. For instance, Sarah can dress herself now and has therapy outside of her "therapy room." Overcoming those obstacles took several years. She can do it, though. She follows simple instructions now, too. Reaching the little milestones is the best reinforcer in the world; it makes all the hardships worthwhile.

Jamie's tips

- Focus on what your child *can* do.
- Keep researching and stay educated.
- Always be on top of what your rights are.
- Never give up hope.

❦

Liz and Eric (14)

On a typical day, Eric wakes up, gets dressed, refuses to eat anything, and takes the bus to school. He's in a special education classroom and this year he'll be in the eighth grade again. After school, he takes a bus to respite until his dad and I get off work. We receive respite services from the Medicaid Developmental Disabilities waiver. This means that Medicaid waives the parents' income in the case of certain developmental disabilities.

Eric has been on the waiver for several years. The way it is set up you get a certain level of care depending on the severity of the child's disability and, accordingly, you get a specific amount of money in your budget for services including respite, therapy, and personal care. We chose to use part of ours for respite.

We have a wonderful respite care provider, Diane. She's provided respite for a lot of different kids; all the families and kids love her. It is extremely helpful that Eric can go to her place after school and we don't have to change our work hours. At other times if we want to clean the house, which Eric isn't very helpful with, or if we want to go to the movies we can call her up and she's almost always available. He goes over to her house and my husband and I get to spend time together. We can actually take Eric out to dinner now sometimes, but for a long time that wasn't the case.

Eric was diagnosed when he was three years old. Over the years we have tried a variety of interventions. Medication was a big help for our family—Prozac for me and other things for Eric. At first, he wasn't sleeping at all so the medication helped him get some rest. That was such a relief for us after years of not being able to get a decent night's sleep. As far as obtaining services, we've been lucky because I'm a professional in a related field (pediatric physical therapy) and my husband makes decent money. I knew the right people and we had the resources to find the help we needed. There were definitely hoops we had to jump through, but we did much better than the majority of families I know.

My husband always says, "Eric will be all right…whatever all right is for Eric." Our primary hope is that he'll be happy. Of course we want him to be able to live as independently as he possibly can, but I doubt he'll ever be able to live on his own. As long as he can find a job doing the things he likes to do and he's got family to oversee things, we know he'll be okay.

Liz's tips

- Go to meetings and training, and learn as much as you can about autism.

- Find other families who are in the same place as you. The only people who can truly understand what you are going through are the people who have done it or are doing it as well. It was a big help for me to have parents whose children were older saying, "It will get better," and "You can survive this."

ॐ

Nicole and Cole (5)

Cole is a blessing first and foremost. He has many strengths, but he also has many weaknesses. Currently we are focusing on improving social interaction and appropriate emotional responses. Cole has few inhibitions, which often leads to difficulties relating to others. He has been diagnosed with Pervasive Developmental Disorder-Not Otherwise Specified (PDD-NOS), although people that have not known him his entire life question the diagnosis. He has progressed a great deal in the last three years.

During the week I work full-time. Since I am a single mother, Cole attends daycare from 8:00 a.m. until 5:00 p.m. Lately, Cole has been getting up with minimal temper tantrums in the morning. He dresses himself and brushes his own teeth with verbal reminders from me. At school, Cole's teachers constantly work on improving his behavior. The staff there work closely with me, cooperating in whatever treatment I initiate. Since Cole has a hard time with respecting personal space, waiting his turn, unanticipated changes in routine, and transitioning from one activity to another, we are constantly experimenting with different ways to help him in those situations.

Recently we set up a "calm down" spot at school for when Cole gets frustrated, overstimulated, or just wants to be alone. This is a partitioned-off area of the classroom referred to as the library. When Cole feels the need to go in there, he tells his teacher and she gets his "heavy blanket," a five-pound weighted blanket, out for him. She allows him to sit in the library until he feels ready to come out. When I pick him up from school he usually throws himself on the floor, kicking, screaming, and crying, but he gets over it fairly quickly. Then we go home and eat dinner, which Cole never finishes because he is so picky. He only wants carbohydrates; it is almost impossible to get him to eat meat and vegetables. During the meal, Cole constantly has to be reminded to lower his voice, wipe his face, use his utensils, and take smaller bites.

After dinner, the kids have some free time to play. Cole is getting tired by this time and his temperament gets worse as the day progresses. He always wants the other kids to do everything his way. If he gets mad for any reason he will attack the other children, especially my two nieces who also live with us. Cole is starting to show some evidence of remorse now when he hurts another child. That is a big step forward for him.

Cole loves to take baths and showers; therefore tantrums are common when he is not able to take one or if he has to get out before he is ready. He washes his hair and body with minimal verbal prompting. After all that, it's time for bed and medicine. He is presently taking Buspar (anti-anxiety) and Melatonin at night to help him fall asleep. He often wakes up in the middle of the night with nightmares and usually wants to sleep in someone else's bed.

Sometimes, it's hard for me to even remember what life was like before Cole. I try not to think about how life used to be because then I start thinking, "Why Cole? He's just a child. It's not fair," and I know that's not a healthy way to think. Mostly I try to focus on the present and positive. My dreams are for Cole to graduate from high school with honors (academically he is very talented), go to his prom with a date, have a girlfriend, have a job that he loves and is good at, and maybe even get married someday. He means the world to me, and if he had to live with me for the rest of his life I'd be content with that, too. I am thankful for the progress he's made just in the past three years, so who knows what the future will bring.

Nicole's tips

- Be your child's advocate; learn as much as you can and communicate with other families. There are people out there going through the same thing, you just have to find them.

- Just hang in there!

CR

Stacy and Brenna (10)

Brenna is a strong-willed, hard-headed, headstrong, affectionate, and loving child. There is never a dull moment when it comes to Brenna. She is always on the move and wanting something to eat (which doesn't necessarily include the act of chewing). Brenna is up at the crack of dawn; she does not know the meaning of sleeping in! She likes to play with her Loving Family dolls and watch movies. She also enjoys looking at books and doing puzzles. We recently purchased a 14-foot trampoline with enclosure for the backyard, and she absolutely loves to go outside and jump.

When Brenna was an infant we noticed something appeared to be wrong. The doctors told us she was developmentally delayed. My husband, Ryan, was in the US Army at the time, stationed in Panama. Due to Brenna's diagnosis he asked for a transfer and we were approved for a compassionate reassignment to the United States.

Our move took us to Colorado Springs, Colorado. We had other friends from inside and outside of the military there, so we were excited to be state side. We got Brenna into therapy, which was just physical therapy (PT) at first. Then our therapist said she thought Brenna would benefit from occupational therapy (OT) and speech therapy (ST) as well. We started going to OT and ST off-base, while still going to PT on-base. It got to be so much that I just switched and had all her therapies in one place. The therapists worked with her under the diagnosis of developmentally delayed, and that was her diagnosis for years. I'm sure if they had realized there was something more that was wrong, we would be further today than we are.

After another move to Indiana, I wasn't sure where to go or whom to talk to about receiving services for Brenna, hence we fell through the cracks. Eventually a neighbor of mine told me about a friend whose little boy had autism. She felt as though this friend of hers could help me and asked if she could share my phone number with her. I welcomed the phone call and listened to what the woman had to say. Following our conversation I was still uncertain how to proceed, so I let the ball drop again.

At that time, Brenna was attending a preschool for developmentally delayed children, and I wasn't happy with how things were progressing. I wanted to know exactly what was wrong and couldn't seem to get a straight answer. I contacted a mental health agency and they reviewed our case. Before long Brenna received a multiple diagnosis of PDD-NOS, Mild Mental Retardation (MMR), and Oppositional Defiant Disorder (ODD). I totally disagreed with the MMR label, protesting: "Look at her! She is *not* retarded!" I went back to see the doctor a few times and he gave me some prescriptions for Brenna.

With no results after a couple of weeks on the medication, to my dismay the doctor doubled the dosage. Within two days of the increase Brenna had a horrible seizure. I had to call 911 because she was not breathing. I was scared; I didn't know any of the neighbors and Ryan was at work. She was admitted to the hospital and remained there for almost two days. Brenna was immediately taken off that medication and put on different medication for seizures (she is still on it today). While monitoring her they found a spike in her brain waves but couldn't tell if the seizure had caused the spike or the other way around. When I returned to the doctor who had prescribed the original medication for a follow-up visit, he said that he could do no more for her and wished me good luck. So there I was once again with nowhere to turn.

Looking for some kind of direction I spoke with our pediatrician. He wanted to know why I wanted a label for Brenna. I told him I wanted to know what was wrong with her and how to deal with it. He referred me to Riley Children's Hospital Developmental Pediatrics Department where they ultimately gave her the diagnosis of autism. The entire process of getting the diagnosis took roughly four years, although it felt like ten!

We tried a variety of treatments after the seizure incident, including Risperdal, Adderall, and a few others that I can't even name, before weaning her off all of them. Now she takes the anti-seizure medication along with Klonopin for anxiety. Brenna receives one hour of speech therapy a week at Riley Children's Hospital. She also receives an hour of speech a month at school as per her Individualized Education Program (IEP).

Stacy's tips

- Stay strong! You have to fight for your child.

- Be your child's voice, and let it be heard. If you don't speak up for them, then who will?

- Believe me, even though it will feel like it, know you are not alone.

- There are other parents out there who are willing to help because they have been there, too.

ભ

Teresa and Nick (9)

Nick is a cool kid. Unless you carry on a conversation with him he's just like any other boy. He likes to ride his bike and his go-kart. He also has a PlayStation 2, but we limit that to weekends. He loves being on the computer and listening to country music.

Seeing our devastation after we received the diagnosis of autism, the head doctor at the Child Study Center was kind enough to call the day after and refer us to the Sooner Start program (Oklahoma's Early Intervention). One of the women who worked at Sooner Start got us interested in ABA. Nick started preschool and an ABA program at the same time. We started with ten hours a week but realized that, to maximize the possibility of success, it was necessary to do the whole full-blown thing. For a few years Nick had 40 hours of therapy a week. Keeping a program like that going is hard, especially in a very small town. Sometimes I used to wish we could live in Dallas where there would have been a larger pool of therapists but here I found people who sincerely cared about my son, and weren't just doing it for the money.

I used to stress because I thought three years old was kind of late to start an intensive program, but it's not. From all the reports, I thought we'd missed that "window of opportunity" they always talk about, but he's getting better all the time. For a while we started to implement the Carbone method, which places emphasis on teaching verbal behavior and difficult to instruct learners, and now we're getting into Relationship Development

Intervention (RDI). Actually, I'm still investigating it, and my husband and I are going to a conference to learn more. Currently I'm on the fence about that particular therapy, but I've always been the type of person to try something if I thought it might be helpful. I never want to look back and say, "If only I'd done this."

Among the treatments we've tried the worst was secretin injections. They had to put Nick to sleep because they couldn't hold him down. He was so little, but five people couldn't keep him still to insert the IV. The secretin was very costly, with no effect. We even tried something called audio integration. I read a book called *Dancing in the Rain* and this mother said the therapy pulled her daughter out of autism. The process involved listening to classical music through expensive headphones to rewire the brain. Needless to say, that didn't work either.

With a somewhat greater degree of success, I tried the no-yeast/GFCF diet. Nick had a yeast overgrowth at one time, which caused him to act drunk. He would even have beer breath. I bought a book by Dr. Bernard Rimland, put Nick on the first stage of the no-yeast diet and the symptoms cleared up almost immediately. We kept him on that for about a year. The first stage is hard enough; I can't imagine doing the whole regimen. I ended up eliminating almost everything from his diet and I was reading food labels everywhere I'd go. It did help though and we don't have that issue any more.

Another positive form of therapy for Nick is swimming. When we first started sensory integration therapy, we were about to go on our first vacation to the beach. We didn't know whether to take Nick or not. He was 18 months old and his brothers were three and four years old. The therapist said to take him and let him sit in the sand and feel the water. He loved the beach! I can't believe we were seriously considering leaving him at home with a sitter as he would have remained shut down the whole time. We have gone to the ocean every year since then. Nick swims like a fish and can stay underwater forever, and he goes into his own world. I don't know what the water does to his senses but it certainly helps. We even used to do some ABA in the pool because simply being in water seems to help Nick pull himself together.

I believe that sensory integration at a young age helped Nick absorb the ABA. At first he wouldn't touch certain things and he wouldn't get into the ball pit. We had a very low step that went out into our garage but he would get down on his hands and knees and crawl down backwards off that step. He had no depth perception whatsoever. They worked on all that—most of the time, therapy looked like playing. I often questioned, "Is that really helping?" but remarkably it did!

When we first started ABA, Nick wouldn't sit down and we had to physically prompt him through everything. He would cry so much during a session he'd fall asleep or end up miserable and exhausted. With ABA drills you work on the same skill for what seems like forever, and you think, "Is he ever going to get it?" Then, all of a sudden, one day he does.

Nick's therapists write notes to me about how each session went and occasionally they will say things like, "Don't pay me today, we didn't get *anywhere!*" I reassure them that the work they do is cumulative. Honestly, of all the therapies we've tried, I know he wouldn't be where he is if it wasn't for ABA. In the more advanced stages of an ABA program, you get away from the therapy table, so a while ago we got rid of the table. We had a whole room specifically set up with white boards on the walls, the whole nine yards—now the therapy room is gone. The day we took those white boards off the wall was one of the best days of my life!

Nick has certainly come a long way. He learned to read on his own and could feed himself from an early age. He's fascinated by facts and things like that, especially country music trivia: his most recent discovery is that Toby Keith is taller than Alan Jackson—to look at them you wouldn't think it—but according to Nick it's true!

Amazingly, Nick has lived up to everything we'd ever wondered if he would do when he was diagnosed. We wondered if he'd ever talk. We wondered if he'd ever be potty trained, tie his shoes, or have a friend. He's done all of them in a timely manner. He even plays the piano and loves being on stage. He won't talk to you one on one, but give him a microphone and you can't keep him quiet. He's done many things we never even dreamed of. On vacation this year we took him to Mexico and he tried snorkeling. As I watched from the boat, I just sat there and cried because he's doing things we never imagined possible. At one time somebody told me, "Raise your expectations and watch him rise to meet the challenge" and he has! I don't mean to brag about everything he's done and proclaim he's cured, he's not. He is great in our eyes though and he's still improving.

Following particularly rough incidents lately, Nick has been saying things like, "Okay, I'm back to normal now!" Then the other day he asked me, "What's not normal?" and I told him some of the things he does that aren't normal, like repeating whole conversations from movies. I wonder if he'll ever talk about being autistic. He doesn't ever mention it so I wonder if he knows he's autistic. He can read though, and I have autism awareness bumper stickers and participate in the autism awareness activities at the state capitol every year, but he never says anything about it. Maybe he knows and doesn't feel the need to talk about it, or he doesn't know how to bring it up. Perhaps I'll never know.

Teresa's tip

- Keep yourself going and stay positive. The kids will be okay if you are okay.

CR

Scott, Susan, and Colton (7)

Colton is very loving, attentive, and outgoing. At this point in his life he likes interacting with other people almost to the point where he is clingy. He prefers to have other people involved in whatever he's doing. We worked with him on that a lot when he was little, and we have struggled to get him to the point where he is starting to initiate things with others. Furthermore, he has episodes of severe frustration and anger, and can go from happily playing one minute to frustrated and striking out the next. His behavior is unpredictable from moment to moment.

With Colton we noticed at a very early age that he ignored us and he would spin repetitively. We were blessed with an excellent daycare provider who had completed her Continuing Education Units (CEUs) in special needs, autism specifically. Every day she would send home a report of how many times each child pooped, what they ate, and at the bottom she would make general comments about what happened that day. Since I am a pack rat by nature, I kept every one of those reports. By going back through his file and looking at what he was doing on a daily basis we started to recognize a pattern in his behavior.

Actually, the daycare provider brought her concerns to our attention around the time when Colton was 14 months old. She said because of the way Colton was acting (i.e. very frustrated, short-fused temper, earth-shattering scream, hitting and aggressive with other kids) she suspected that he had some autistic tendencies. We started reading back through all the notes she had taken and saw that there were numerous aggression issues that often escalated into violent temper tantrums. We took that information and began to research on the Internet.

As we surfed the web we found a myriad sites dealing with autism. Some of the sites contained checklists like "Ten Symptoms of an Autistic Child." We'd review the list and, out of the ten traits, Colton would have seven or eight. Then we'd discover another list of 20 symptoms and Colton would have 15 of them.

At 18 months we put Colton on a herbal regimen and kept a journal every day detailing how he was acting, what he did, what dosage of herbs he was receiving, and his reaction to them. Believe it or not, he did phenomenally well for about six months. The herbs really helped—at that time we were using valerian root for anger control, vitamin B12, and another herb to increase awareness.

After the initial period, the herbs started to lose their effectiveness, and we maxed out on the dosage someone his age and weight could safely take. We were starting to see some of the aggression return. We hired a live-in nanny right before we left on a three-day business trip. While we were gone, she decided she didn't like our parenting skills so she changed Colton's entire routine. He went berserk. When we got home all the furniture had been removed from his room, she had locked him in, and there were dents in all his walls from where he had been throwing his toys. Colton was violently out of control.

Luckily, when we got back from the trip that Friday afternoon, we were able to reach a psychiatrist who prescribed medication for him. The drug he prescribed was very effective; however, it took several days before it had a substantial effect. For about a week neither Scott nor I could go to work because we had to stay with Colton day and night. All he tried to do during that time was self-destruct. His behavior was incredibly violent, especially considering he was only two and a half years old at the time. Scott would have to hug him to restrain him and it was all he could do to hold on to him. Imagine this big 6' 3", 280-pound man struggling to contain this little boy; it was everything he could do to stop Colton from hurting himself. A week later we finally had our son back.

We went back to the doctor and told him Colton was getting thrown out of daycare almost daily. He had a tendency to pick up one of those heavy wooden play kitchens at random and chuck it three or four feet across the room. He also periodically threw chairs. We'd have to go pick him up so he wouldn't endanger the other children. The doctor recommended a drug that researchers had been experimenting with for autistic children. The FDA had done some preliminary trials but had not fully endorsed it at the time. The drug was Risperdal. Colton had used Risperdal for several years when they came out with a study that declared it was the greatest thing since sliced bread. We were fortunate that we got him on it as early as we did because it made a tremendous difference in his life and ours. Basically, the drug enabled him to control his aggressive emotions so he could start to develop as a person. Colton's psychoanalysts and the doctor are now in agreement that, by the age of 12, he won't need any medications at all, and we will hardly be able to tell he's autistic.

The doctors also tell us time and again that they believe the biggest influence on where he is today is how early we got involved. From the beginning we have tried everything within reason we thought would help. On the Internet someone suggested getting a trampoline because autistics use repetitive motion. So since Colton's biggest thing was jumping and spinning we got a trampoline. Another thing we were told is that autistics struggle with proprioceptive input because the neurons in their joints don't fire properly. That got us doing a lot of physical work with heavy bags and things like that to give him tactile and sensory input all over his body. We also got him a ball pit and swings; research told us to try these types of things to increase his proprioceptive input and joint compression. We're a very physical family anyway so we tickle and wrestle a lot, and we came to find out that was exactly what he needed.

All these interventions, combined with the input of the doctor and his willingness to work with us, have really made a huge difference in Colton. He was very introverted when he was younger. He did his own thing and wouldn't play with his brothers. Now he's completely the opposite.

One of the things we've never done is keep him on a rigid routine. We totally disagree with that, at least where Colton is concerned. Our life has been total chaos ever since my husband and I met. If our son had to be on a specific schedule he would never survive in our household. The best part of not having a set routine is that it allows him to be flexible with change. Colton has always struggled with transitions—either he wants to continue an enjoyable activity or he doesn't want to do the new activity. I am confident that if we had him on a strict schedule we wouldn't be as able to function as a family.

Our plans are constantly in flux. We could be going to the grocery store one minute and then decide to stop and get some gas. Colton used to get upset about minor deviations from routine. "We're not going to Wal-Mart. Why aren't we going to Wal-Mart?" he'd scream. I'd say, "Colton, we are going to stop and get gas first and then we're going to Wal-Mart." Now he can go with the flow and say it's okay to himself. We've worked with him on it over the years. We tell him we're going to go do this but that we've got to do some other things first; so he doesn't freak out when it's been a couple of hours and he still hasn't gotten to do what he wanted to do. He'll make comments like, "This is taking a long time. When are we going to do this?" He asks appropriate questions instead of throwing a fit. We've also had a great deal of family upheaval since Colton was born, including moving at least ten times—following a strict routine would have been impossible.

Having Colton in our lives has changed us for the better. I am a total workaholic and I would probably work 20-hour days if I didn't have somebody like Colton in my life to force me to appreciate my family. Colton makes me appreciate the little things in life like hearing him sing along with a song on the radio, watching him play with his brothers, or seeing him walk up to a little girl he doesn't even know and say, "Hi, how are you? Will you play with me?" I no longer take things like that for granted.

Susan and Scott's tips

- Research. Use the Internet with a grain of salt. Beware of "miracle cures."

- Use every tool you can find to help get your child as far as he can go.

- Pray a lot!

- Stay strong as a husband and wife. Feed on each other's strengths and appreciate each other.

- Realize we're all human, and you are going to have moments when you don't understand what's happening or why it's happening.

- Have faith—no matter how bad things are, find the good in them. Look for the silver lining because it's there.

- Appreciate the little things.

ॐ

A professional's perspective: Jennifer Crawford, M.Ed., Board Certified Associate Behavior Analyst

Five years ago I was teaching Speech and Debate in a public school when a parent informed me that she wanted to enroll her son—who had Asperger's Syndrome—in my class. I didn't hesitate to accept him, and he became an involved participant in my class. Something about him made me take a liking to him and made me curious to learn more about his disorder.

When I saw an episode of *Nightline* featuring autism and ABA I said to my husband, "Can you give me a year to be successful doing that?" He agreed and I quit my full-time position to work 20 hours a week with a drastic reduction in salary. My goal was to learn all there was to know about ABA from the ground up. The experiment was a success and I ended up co-founding an ABA-based school in Virginia.

From early on other professionals encouraged my progress because the principles and practice of ABA seemed to come naturally. Quickly my gift became my passion. I love seeing the "Eureka…I got it!" look in the kids' eyes when they master a new concept and everything connects. My favorite part is the first time a completely non-verbal child laughs. That's the kind of thing that makes me cry in the car on the way home at the end of the day. The small successes and breakthroughs make all the struggles and hours of repetition worthwhile.

My approach is to treat each child as an individual and consider the whole child rather than compartmentalizing specific needs. Using ABA as the core, I bring in things like sensory integration techniques and music as necessary. The biggest challenge for me is dealing with the occasional feelings of disappointment that occur when a particular child doesn't achieve something I want so much for them to accomplish. I know I expect a lot from them, and high expectations can't always be reached—but that doesn't stop me from trying. Basically, my expectations make me work harder to find different ways to teach something if a child just doesn't get it.

Families who are best able to cope with the frustrations of having a child with a developmental disorder are those who are able to live in the moment. The ones who are always looking ahead and wondering, "Will my child ever be able to do this or that?" are continually frustrated and tend to get stuck in a "Why me?" mentality. Parents who are able to look at their child and accept what their current needs are, and help the child to work on what needs to improve in the present, are those that are most successful. If a child is three years old, don't get bogged down with what he or she will be capable of at age 12 or 20; doing that is counterproductive.

Some families seem to want and expect their children to change overnight. In the case of autism there is no magic bullet, just a lot of effort and hard work. These families get frustrated with a particular method and switch philosophies at the drop of a dime. Since one of the biggest developmental needs of children with autism and Asperger's is consistency, my advice to parents out there is to do your research, choose a plan of action, hire the best people you can, and then have the faith to let it go. Don't overanalyze the situation, make a decision and get involved in making whatever you choose successful.

I've worked in several states and the one thing I've noticed is that availability and access to resources varies. Here in Texas, we are ranked 48th or 49th in funding for special education, but it still matters where you live and what school your child attends. Frankly, it's the parents themselves that can make the most difference. When a group of parents unite and push and fight to make changes or receive a new service they have tremendous power to make a lasting difference for all children involved.

Jennifer's tips

- Do what you know is best for your child.
- Even if "they" have tons of degrees, don't be scared or intimidated into doing something you are not comfortable with for you or your family.

Jennifer can be contacted at jennifer@thelearninglane.com.

SOMETHING TO TALK ABOUT

1. There are so many therapies out there, how do you know where to start? Which intervention do you believe worked the best for you and why?

2. Where is the best place to start to find money for therapy and related services? Is there any way to get insurance companies to help cover the cost of treatments?

3. There are many drugs used in relation to autism. What are the benefits and side effects of some of the most commonly used drugs?

4. How do I go about setting up a home therapy program?

5. We qualify and receive funding for services but we are unhappy with the service providers. How can I go about getting improved services for my child?

REFLECTION ACTIVITY

Review notes from a therapist or doctor. Record your thoughts and feelings about how your child has progressed in the past six months/year/five years.

3.

School Daze: Our Experiences Navigating the Educational System

Becca and Alex (4)

Alex has attended school for the past two years. I'm an involved mom and I knew that our district would allow him to start preschool early if there was space, so I pushed for that. He had about three months of school during the first year and just completed his second full year. Because of a late birthday he's not old enough for kindergarten yet, but he's ready.

We've tried several types of classroom. Initially Alex was placed in an integrated classroom with 11 other children with various special needs and several typical students. Unfortunately the chaos of that classroom was too much for him; with all the kids, teachers, aides, and therapy staff coming in and out he started to have seizures because he was so overstimulated. I fought for and received an aide for him the next year since the school administrators didn't want him in the self-contained classroom because he is so verbal. I understood their argument and I said, "Fine, but I'm not going to have the kid coming home after two hours falling apart and having seizures. That's not acceptable." So the aide came and Alex was able to manage better.

During that school year we ended up moving within the same town but to a new school district. Since Alex was going to be in class for only a few weeks the officials there recommended we try him in the self-contained program because of all his sensory issues. We put him in the self-contained classroom and he was like a totally different kid when he came home from school. He participated in family activities because he wasn't overstimulated and could function. By the time he begins first or second grade we're shooting for a mainstream classroom, but I think it's going to take a bit more time for him to mature enough to handle the sensory overload that occurs in a regular classroom environment.

In the area of Arizona where we live the population is booming, so there could be as many as 35 kids in a kindergarten class and there is no way Alex could handle that. I don't want to set him up to fail. When schools are saying, "Here, we'll try you in this and once you've failed we will do what is adequate for you," due to financial constraints, we can't just sit back and agree. Unless we as parents take a proactive course we lose all that time that our children could be improving. It makes absolutely no sense, except to the one who is watching the dollar signs. Fortunately we found what works for Alex and he's doing okay.

Becca's tips

- Fight to get proper educational services from the beginning.
- Look beyond the label.
- Love your children for who they are.
- Be gentle with yourself.

ᗣ

Chuck and Kyle (9)

The very first teacher my son ever had pulled me aside one day in the parking lot and said, "If I were you I honestly would ask for about 800 more things for my son. You better get a backbone quickly!" From that point on I did.

In the part of Virginia where we live we are in the fastest-growing county in the USA, so the school system has huge growth problems. Special needs kids always tend to get pushed to the back of the bus anyway, but here even the normal kids are getting pushed around. Every single year Kyle was going to a different school for his educational needs. For a kid that doesn't like breaks in routine, going to a new school every year meant that we were losing more ground than we were gaining. All the switching around was getting to be annoying; by the time Kyle was in first grade he had already been in four schools! We hadn't moved—the county just kept moving the location of his program.

I recommend that parents compile a list of everything they want from their school district for their child, and make sure each item gets on the Individualized Education Program (IEP). Then I instruct them, "If the school district says no to a request due to lack of funding, say, 'That's against the law.' If the school district says a particular service is not available say, 'That's against the law, too!'" I also tell them, "If you are not completely satisfied with anything that is written on an IEP get up and leave the meeting right then and there." You'd be surprised how many school administrators will have a nuclear meltdown the moment you do that.

Even if you are satisfied with the outcome of the meeting but disagree with a specific point, be sure to write that on the IEP. That paperwork is your only legal recourse if there is a problem in the future. If you don't like something, write "I don't like that" next to the specific point in question so if you ever end up going to court you'll have proof. To me, those papers are more important than the paperwork that bought my house.

Being aware of the laws regarding special education I wrote up Kyle's IEP stating, "If and when you move the program, we need two to three weeks before school starts to be able to transition Kyle without any problem." That simple statement in his IEP paid off in a major way. Right before the beginning of the very next school year they told us that Kyle would be attending a new school because the old school was being refurbished. Construction was behind schedule, and they said they wouldn't be able to let the kids into the building at all prior to the first day of classes. I said, "Fine, according to the IEP guidelines I can issue a stay-put clause, which means he stays in his current school." The county had a problem with that because they'd already moved the teachers from his program into the new school. Even the classroom they used the previous year had been taken over by another program. Legally I had them cornered.

At the same time all this commotion was going on with the public school system, a woman from the local Association for Retarded Citizens (Arc) noticed the problems autism was creating in the county and she was setting up a separate school. I was pushing the school district to allow Kyle to attend even though I never remotely believed we stood a chance of getting him in due to the cost. This was going to be a private school where the cost would run to $60,000–$80,000 per year for each student to attend. After putting some pressure on the county as far as their legal obligations regarding building changes, they finally admitted defeat and agreed to send Kyle to the private school at their expense.

This school is the first Kyle has attended for more than a year. He's about to start his second year and he'll be there again the year after next. The program is slated for children until they reach 12 years old or, in other words, the end of sixth grade. Beyond that we're trying to figure out how to make it grow, otherwise Kyle will go back into the public school system.

For most people it is virtually impossible to get a county to pay for a school like that. Only children who are very severely affected will ever get placed out of the school system. My son is one of the few who is completely non-verbal. However, it was anticipating the county's next move, rather than any inherent characteristic of Kyle's, that got him where he is now. In this case, I predicted their moves correctly and won.

Ironically, the only time Kyle ever received an autism label was from the county education program. I prefer the diagnosis of "severely disabled," which qualifies him to receive more services here in this state. During a routine re-evaluation, no one could dispute the classification of severely disabled so he was relabeled. Kyle is definitely not showing up for any statistics on autism, but I know what's wrong. I'll take whatever label I can get to provide him with the best possible care.

Chuck's tips

- Learn to play the politics. Understand the laws and your rights. Don't go into a battle unless you're fully prepared.

- Try to find a balance between educational and medical interventions. You might need to do only one or the other, or a balance of both. Don't just try a medical intervention and let your child's brain turn to mush: research educational practices, try a variety of things and find what works for your particular child.

Chuck can be contacted through Unlocking Autism (Virginia) or at www.autismva.org.

CR

Connie and Chris (15)

When Chris was five, we worked for a long time to get him to respond to the question, "What's your name?" instead of just echoing and repeating the question. We were at the park one day playing with some other little kids and they were all having a grand time. Inevitably, one of the children stopped and said, "What's your name?" I was literally halfway off the bench, prepared to intervene, when he said it, "My name is Chris," with no prompt, completely independently. I wanted to jump and scream and cry and carry on, but there were other people around who I'm positive had no clue about the miraculous event that had just transpired. I was truly ready to stand on top of the bleachers shouting at the top of my lungs, *"He did it! Look what he did!"* Typical parents don't realize what a blessing it is when their child is able to answer that simple question. Moments later my bubble of excitement burst when the boy turned around and asked him, "What school do you go to?" and I thought, "Oh, damn. I know what we need to work on next."

Before Chris entered kindergarten I left things up to the school to deal with, as our doctor suggested. Around that time there was a lady who was visiting the preschool classes to look for students who qualified for a special program. She wanted him in a class at her elementary school, but in order to qualify Chris had to be relabeled autistic instead of having Pervasive Developmental Disorder (PDD). When I heard the word autism I freaked out. At that point I began to question what all these labels meant. I started reading and educating myself and learned about the spectrum—after that the new label wasn't so scary.

Meeting that teacher was the best thing that happened to Chris because the school he was in hadn't been doing much in the way of intervention. When he went to this new elementary school they knew all about Applied Behavioral Analaysis (ABA) therapy and Floor Time. Moreover, Greenspan and Lovaas were household names for them. They were able to implement all the different techniques and therapies with him right in his classroom.

Moreover, the teachers were able to offer me lots of book titles to further my education. While it wasn't an autism class (it was considered part of the moderately mentally handicapped program) I felt extremely fortunate to find a school where the teachers had a clue. During Chris's first year there he turned around so drastically that they began talking about mainstreaming him. The success we experienced had everything to do with getting him into the right program with the right teachers who knew how to use effective therapies and technologies with him.

I suppose I was spoiled in a sense when Chris was in elementary school. The teachers and staff got to know him, and they taught me about how to help him be successful. The best advice they gave me was, "If you expect him to do a little bit, that's all he's ever going to do. Even if he can do a mountain of work, he'll only ever meet your expectations. If your expectations are low then he'll do exactly what you expect." They recognized Chris had so much potential and capability and set their expectations accordingly.

As Chris proceeded to middle school and high school, I always made certain the administrators were aware that it was my choice where he was enrolled. I thoroughly checked out the programs that were available at all the schools in the surrounding area. There were some schools I would never have sent him to. One school was so horrendous I was crying when I left.

The only thing the students were working on was living skills; no academics were covered at all. I thought to myself, "Over my dead body will my son go there!"

I looked very carefully at the remaining three high schools nearby to see what they offered before selecting one for Chris. One school automatically got axed. I went to the open house and the teachers didn't have the first clue where the special education program was located. I wondered, "What kind of school are you running where the teachers don't even know where the special education department is? Where are you hiding these children?" Even though the regular education program appeared to be wonderful, the fact that the teachers didn't know about special education overshadowed any good things that might have been taking place there.

For the other schools I took a day off work to visit and observe. At the second school when I asked about parent involvement the special education teacher got agitated about my question. I don't know if she'd had a bad day or I'd touched a raw nerve but it really set her off. Then I asked her about IEPs and goals, and she said, "We don't like to have more than eight goals on the IEPs because we don't have the staff to collect all the data." I was astounded. I couldn't believe anybody would actually admit that to me.

Finally I went to visit the school Chris actually ended up attending. No one there had any idea I had a child in special education, I just went as a regular parent. During the open house all the teachers were having a great time. They were open-minded and they knew where the special education department was (and fortunately it was not in the basement). Later, during my half-day visit, everyone was accommodating and concerned with our needs, asking, "What can we do to help? What questions do you need answered? What is Chris like?" I also learned that the principal at that school was very strict about discipline and he conveyed that message to the parents and students right from the beginning.

Presently, Chris has just completed his freshman year of high school. Aside from the academic program, one of my biggest concerns when choosing a school was bullying. The elementary school had offered Chris a protected environment. Everybody knew everybody else. They also did an excellent job mainstreaming and reverse mainstreaming. If Chris happened to be walking down the hallway flapping his hands nobody took any notice because, "That's just Chris. No big deal. That's what he does." At middle school and high school level, bullying became a major concern. The staff and administrators of Chris's current school quickly put my mind at ease. According to them bullying would absolutely not be tolerated.

We had a minor incident early in the school year and the staff did a good job taking care of it and making sure the kids stopped. A group of boys were trying to get him to "flip the bird" and he wasn't sure what that meant. His instincts told him it was probably something naughty but he wasn't sure. He came home and discussed the problem with me and I told him he made a good choice not to participate. Of course, I also called the teacher and explained what happened, and the situation was quickly rectified.

I feel confident that if Chris ever has another issue there are supportive people he can go to and he will be safe. I know if something happens, the staff will resolve things immediately. If there were any change in how things were dealt with or I was unsatisfied in any way with Chris's treatment I would have no qualms about pulling him out of school. We have worked so hard on his self-esteem there is no way I'm going to jeopardize that progress because of a lack of care on some administrator's part.

In addition to structured academic activities I believe in incidental teaching: whatever comes up, let's sit down and work on it. Recently Chris became fascinated by Japanese animation and suddenly I'm bombarded with questions like, "Where's Japan?" I pulled the maps out, and we had a lesson in world geography on the spot. I probably gave him more information than he wanted, but when we were done he definitely knew where Japan was. He was interested and motivated, and the timing was right for learning so that's what we did.

I have always taken an active role in Chris's education and progress. When he was little someone told me to get him out of the house and expose him to everything. You really never know when something is going to click with him and he's going to get it. So it was always my belief that we needed to do things like go to the park, restaurants, and the zoo, and encourage him to be interested in things. Over the years there were many things that didn't click, but we kept trying. Some people question my attempts, but to me I've always been of the opinion, "Why wouldn't you put the effort in? Why would you have a kid if you weren't going to put the time in to the whole process of helping them learn and giving them what they need?"

Connie's tip

- Remember there is an unwritten policy in schools that states, "If the parents don't ask we won't tell." There are some excellent programs out there that could help your child that you are not aware of. Ask lots of questions and keep asking.

ᗄ

Corinne and C.J. (12)

Invariably C.J. is late for school. He rushes around to find his trumpet, books, and folders for all six classes. From second to fifth grade he had a full-time aide, but C.J. never knew because he was classified as a classroom aide. He's come a long way. C.J. attends a public school because the private schools in our area just don't have the resources he needs. At first school was difficult because each day began with a different "special" (music, art, library, etc.). The students would have a quick morning meeting in the classroom and then immediately go somewhere else. The schedule was so disruptive for C.J. we finally had it written in his IEP that he could miss specials every day and come in an hour later without being marked tardy. After we made the change, everything went more smoothly. When he began second grade he sat under the desk, now he goes to classes by himself.

We make sure to meet all of his teachers during the summer so the transition won't be so difficult. Now that he's in middle school, he changes classes throughout the day. The administration agreed to let us put a piece of numbered blue construction paper on each of C.J.'s classrooms to correspond with the class periods so that if he ever gets disoriented he can find his way. In fact, each of the teachers in those rooms was given a copy of his complete class schedule so they can direct him to the correct classroom if he becomes confused.

So far, the system has worked perfectly and has allowed him to be self-sufficient. As C.J. gets older, doing things without assistance has become a lot more important to him. When he realized that the classroom aide was actually there for him he rebelled and said, "What do I have to do to get rid of him?" So, with the stipulation that he would turn his work in on time, get to all of his classrooms on his own, and be prepared for class, he was able to be on his own.

In the fourth grade, C.J. made friends with three other boys in his class and fortunately they have been together ever since. One of the boy's mothers saw that C.J. was a little different and encouraged her son to get to know him. The boys all enjoy the same activities and the others accept him for what he has to offer. Over the years they've even helped him stay on task in class when there's no aide around.

Our attitude with the schools has always been to focus on C.J.'s abilities rather than his deficits. Having a background in working with children with special needs, I also made sure the diagnosis he received was PDD-NOS rather than autism or Asperger's. With PDD on his records it helps to ensure he is treated as an individual, rather than a label, because people just don't know what PDD is.

When I explain something about C.J.'s needs to a teacher, we approach the situation by saying, "Here's the symptom, and here's what we're trying to change. This is what hasn't worked, and here's what we'd like to try now," and enlist her help. In almost every case, teachers have been receptive to this approach. I think they feel like we're in this as a team.

Consequently, C.J. has excelled in school. At the end of this past school year he won one of four band awards, made the A-B honor roll, and participated actively as a member of the chess club. He also attends gifted and advanced classes. I know if he had been given a different label someone along the way might have told him, "You don't have to learn those things." C.J. is an extremely bright young man and we are proud of his progress; nothing gets in his way!

Corinne's tips

- Hook up with others who understand and are dealing with the same issues you are.

- Find someone else who is already doing what you want to try with your own child and use them as your model.

 beginornament

Lynn and Cassidy (21)

My son Cassidy has billions of questions. He talks constantly. When he was little, they always said his major problem is he can't talk, so they taught him and he hasn't shut up yet. Thanks a lot! On a typical day, he eats breakfast, listens to music, and messes around on the computer. That's about it.

Cassidy spends a ton of time on the computer. In fact, that's just about all he does. He crashed the first two or three computers we had because he used them so much. We had to replace the hard drives and everything; they wore out from overuse. During that process, Cassidy became a fabulous computer technician. He even tried to start his own computer repair service, but it's very difficult for him to manage all the details that go into running a business. We hope one day he'll be able to get a full-time job doing what he loves, but so far he hasn't had much luck. Most troubleshooter jobs require you to have transportation, and he can't drive. In the meantime Cassidy is here with me, all day, every day.

Last year instead of graduating with his class, Cassidy stayed in school an extra year. The school district allowed him to volunteer in the computer lab at the elementary school just a couple blocks from our house. The kids loved him and the staff thought he was terrific. Even though Cassidy can be difficult to work with at times, the computer teacher absolutely adored him. He had this amazing gift to tune into the kids when they were having trouble, and he was able to show them how to do things in a way they understood. My husband and I find that particularly interesting since he doesn't pay a bit of attention to the foster kids we've had around our house.

We adopted Cassidy when he was 16 months old, but he has lived with us since he was 3 months old. When he turned two the pediatrician said he suspected Cassidy had ADHD. Later, when he started preschool I noticed he never played with the other kids, but he still didn't seem all that different from them to me. The best way I could describe how he appeared is "quirky."

Back when Cassidy was diagnosed with autism his situation was very unique. He was also diagnosed with Tourette's Syndrome. Repeatedly, I was told that it was my fault that he wasn't developing normally. It would have helped me to know there were other people who had the same challenges. Most of the professionals blamed me for his problems. Even though I was 35 years old, and confident in my own abilities, regardless of what was wrong with Cassidy everything was my fault. The only thing I ever wanted to be in my life was a mother, but I couldn't have any biological children. I couldn't seem to get anything right with this one either. Looking back, I can see that God was preparing me to have the tenacity to raise Cassidy.

From the time Cassidy entered kindergarten until he began high school he was never in the same school two years running. There was absolutely no consistency in his education. Early on he was identified as "potentially learning disabled" due to the fact that he was a foster child and because of the intervention he received for the developmental delays he had early in life. His first year of school was also the first year of inclusion within the school district. As far as the administration of the program was concerned, things were a nightmare. There was a lot of resistance toward mainstreaming special needs children and Cassidy could sense it. By April, the tension was so great Cassidy blew up at school and they expelled him. He's the only kid in town that has ever been expelled from kindergarten! For the rest of the year a teacher came out to our house once a week for what they termed "homeschool."

In first grade, they put Cassidy in a special education class at a different school and he was very successful. For second grade he was in yet another school. He was doing perfectly. His teacher called me every Friday to rave about what a great kid he was and how he did his work every day. She was tickled with his progress. The following summer we had to switch up some medication he was using and everything went downhill after that. He became extremely aggressive—he totally destroyed everything in his room, and he threw things at me. He was screaming up to six hours a day. We switched medicines again before he went back to school, but it was too little too late. In the first few days of school he pushed an aide. Remember this was a child who had previously functioned normally in a classroom. As we continued to alter the dosage, things eventually got so bad that we admitted him to the crisis unit at the regional medical center. Finally, the medication was corrected and Cassidy got better. He wasn't great, but better.

At every step I felt the guilt of not having done what I felt was right. Instead, I had trusted the professionals who supposedly knew what they were doing. If I had followed my gut feeling Cassidy wouldn't have suffered so much. The scary part is that he remembers this experience at school very well, which is the most disturbing aspect to me.

As the school year progressed issues related to the Tourette's Syndrome became increasingly prominent. The teachers weren't trained or prepared to handle someone with Cassidy's problems, and it seemed to them that he was making noises just to get attention. The punishments got so bad I removed him from the school. The staff thought that his behavior was intentional so if they punished him more severely he would understand what was and was not appropriate. Of course, the more he anticipated what would happen when he did behave a certain way, the more his stress increased, and in turn the more he behaved like that. Cassidy was trapped in a vicious cycle.

When I taught Cassidy at home, I didn't see behavior problems to that extent. Sure, he was quirky, but if he knew what the routine was, and if I told him what to expect ahead of time he was great. It wasn't until my daughter Kelsey (also adopted) got older that I saw that most of what Cassidy did was not so terribly abnormal—kids make noises. However, other boys and girls learn not to do it in front of the teacher. Autistic kids don't know the difference; they never get it.

When Cassidy re-entered school in the fourth grade I was determined he would be successful. I requested a meeting with the entire staff of the school to discuss what we were going to do and how we were going to deal with him. A representative from the Intermediate Unit (IU), the special education department, came out and explained to everyone the particulars of autism and Tourette's, and the methods that are most productive when working with these kids. I could almost see a light go on in their heads! The teacher immediately began to change how she responded to Cassidy and it made all the difference. I also insisted that Cassidy not have a personal assistant—another assistant could be in the classroom but no one would be specifically assigned to him. The teacher, the assistant, and the additional assistant would all be adults in the classroom if he needed help but he wouldn't have someone sitting at his elbow prodding him every second of his life. That year was very successful.

During the first week of middle school, Cassidy was suspended for screaming in the hallways. Unfortunately, the teacher sent him to the gym by himself without clothes or instructions what to do. When he got to the locker room some boy told him that he had to take off his clothes. Misunderstanding, his response was to run back to the classroom screaming and he was suspended. Several weeks later, after everything was cleared up and Cassidy was back at school, he got mad at his assistant and threw a shoe at her. Needless to say he was expelled from school and the police were called. We almost went to court, but a deal was made where he had to accept responsibility for his actions, write a letter of apology, and do some community service. He still didn't understand though. Afterward he was secluded in a tiny classroom for the rest of the school year. His only interaction with other humans was with his one-on-one teacher.

In order to prevent further difficulties, the psychologist from the IU came and looked over the situation to assess the best way to help Cassidy. Instead of telling Cassidy, "You can't scream any place in this building ever, that's not what you do in school," he told him, "If you feel really frustrated, this is the place you can scream, but you must close the door and not bother other people." Cassidy did it—he could do it because they gave him *options*. If he needed to go outside and take a break or take a walk to cool down and get himself back together, it was okay. Once they gave him some alternatives he did really well.

For sixth grade I refused to put Cassidy in the Emotional Support classroom again. Through conversations with administrators we discovered that he qualified for the Neurologically Impaired (NI) class with a wonderful little old lady teacher who had been working with mentally disabled children for over 30 years. She understood his needs. For the first time, Cassidy got to go out for classes like Art, Music, and Tech Ed. He even built a bird house and took a computer class. He did it all and was incredibly successful! Up until that point, I would leave him at a school at 8:30 in the morning and often, by 9:00, they would call me to come get him. Every other day he was coming home for one reason or another. That year I think the only time I had to pick him up early was during a two-day period while they were doing state assessment tests and they didn't want him to disturb the other kids with Tourette's noises or walking down the hall or something. Other than that he did marvelously.

Much to our satisfaction Cassidy attended the same high school all four years. His teacher was a big hippie guy from California. He was laid back and joked a lot with the kids. He understood that kids with autism don't get the subtleties of language so made things simple so they could understand. He was real easy to laugh and slow to anger—a perfect match. Cassidy is still friends with him today. Ultimately, high school was a great success.

Cassidy always asks, "Why do I have to be like this?" and "Why am I the only person like this?" I tell him, "God has a plan for our lives and this is yours. You impact people and change their lives." Of course, that doesn't make it any easier when you're the only 21-year-old who can't go anywhere on Saturday night when everybody else is having dates and girlfriends.

Cassidy is quirky. He stands too close to other people; he talks too fast; he asks too many questions, and never listens. He can't change it though because he doesn't understand what "it" is. I've always treated Cassidy as though he is perfectly normal, because he is perfectly normal, for him. Nobody ever said God was going to make us all the same. Cassidy may be quirky, but we enjoy him for who he is.

Lynn's tips

- Read everything you can find.
- Believe only what feels right.
- Don't let anybody tell you that "you have to" do anything.

$$\text{\Large ❧}$$

Sophie and Ben (10)

I attended an IEP meeting back in February. Usually I sit across from the school district representative, however this time we were crammed into a little room so I ended up sitting next to her. As we discussed each service Ben received she would type the team's recommendations into her laptop computer. After each decision was entered, a separate page would pop up with the total dollar amount per school year. I thought Ben was a pretty expensive kid to have in their school district, but when I saw the final total I nearly fell off my chair. Incredibly, it cost over $25,000 for one school year!

Obviously, the level of help is great here and this district is trying to provide what is best for the kids.

In the beginning I had to fight to get the regular doctors to point me in the right direction. There are so many types of services available here in Pennsylvania but at first no one would tell me anything about how to get them. Everything was very hush-hush. Finally someone told me to check out Early Intervention, but they didn't give me a phone number or an address. I felt like a detective searching for clues on how to help my son.

One of the first meetings we had was with a special education teacher. When I brought Ben into the classroom he was fine but once he saw the teacher he started screaming his head off and hid under her desk. Over the screaming she acknowledged that she would do her best to help. Her face seemed to betray a feeling of dread—and this was from a seasoned professional who had been teaching for over 15 years. No doubt she had seen it all, until now. He screamed throughout our entire conversation. Finally, we dragged him out from under her desk because the speech therapist wanted to evaluate him. No luck that day!

Oddly enough, Ben remained in that classroom during both years of preschool and loved the teacher. He entered kindergarten on schedule the following year. At school he learned "The Pledge of Allegiance." Although he still couldn't speak very well, I could tell what it was. I brought him back see his old teacher and said, "Come on Ben, let's say the pledge," and he did. She couldn't believe how much progress he had made in a year.

Several months ago, the psychologist who re-evaluated Ben accidentally left out the diagnosis of autism. The school officials were unable to do anything for Ben until we had him put the diagnosis back in the report. He was new to the job and didn't realize the significance of that one word: autism. Paperwork is a big issue with the schools and you have to make sure to state each time there is an evaluation where your child falls on the spectrum. Ben continues to progress on the spectrum: when we first began everything he was in the severe range, now his symptoms are more under control. One of the psychiatrists mentioned that he might end up having Asperger's Syndrome. At this point, I don't care what they call it as long as he can function.

Actually Ben has a dual diagnosis of autism and mental retardation, which I found it really hard to accept at first. How can they expect someone who can't communicate to take a test that truly indicates their intelligence? However, it qualifies him to receive additional services so now I just view it as another part of the paperwork. I know he'll never be a rocket scientist, but Ben's labels don't make us love him any less.

For the longest time Ben was in what the school system called an Autistic Support Classroom. Recently we moved to a different district so he is now enrolled in what they call Multiple Disabilities Support. Before we switched schools, all the children in his classroom were autistic spectrum kids. Here they are grouped on the basis of functional level, although the diagnosis may differ somewhat. I think half of the kids in his class have a PDD-NOS diagnosis. I actually prefer the set-up he has now, because there are only six or seven kids in the classroom and as many staff members; basically it's one on one. The structure is very beneficial because Ben needs a high level of assistance.

Ben thrives on routine, so going to school provides him with the structure he needs. Right now they are working on harder things at school, so he's been having some difficulty. He'll tell me school is boring and that he doesn't want to go. However, once he realizes I'm not going to give in and let him stay home he'll decide that he wants to go. He stares out the window repeating, "Where's my bus?" in anticipation until it arrives.

Sophie's tips

- Keep being the squeaky wheel.
- Talk to *everyone* and ask lots of questions.
- Take advantage of the Internet; there is a wealth of information available.
- If you know in your gut something is not quite right—*investigate*. Don't wait! The earlier you start, the easier it is to establish language.
- Be aggressive and demand what you need.

CR

Theresa and Josiah (7)

Josiah's days fluctuate so dramatically there is no middle ground for him. He is a picture of extremes. One moment he can be the most loving, gentle, concerned, and considerate child, and the next he is in a rage, aggressive, and out of control. Prior to starting medication, Josiah would sleep only two to four hours a day, now he generally sleeps between six to seven hours every night.

We can always tell when Josiah wakes up because all the doors upstairs slam as he closes each and every one. He then lumbers down the stairs with loud "thump-thumps" on the steps and plops himself down, sitting Indian style on the couch. If I am already sitting on the couch, he will snuggle up as close as he can. If I am not there yet, I will hear, "Mommmm. You come sit down!" as he points to the spot on the couch next to him. Josiah's attachment to me is very strong. I joked with the doctor during his delivery that he had his hands on my pelvic bone and was pushing himself back into the womb. Sometimes it seems like he can't get close enough to me and would crawl under my skin if he could. After about 15 minutes on the couch, he is up and running for the rest of the day.

Breakfast is often a combination of toast, dry cereal, popsicles, ice cream, and cookies. He eats green popsicles almost non-stop to combat the dry mouth he experiences as a side effect of his psychiatric medications. I run daycare from my home so with each additional family arriving, Josiah becomes more excited. He has no concept of personal space so frequently hugs, sits on, and pushes others in ways that to him may seem gentle and friendly but to other children probably seems more like being hit by a freight train.

Josiah shifts from one activity to the next, often listening to the television while he eats, and doing something else simultaneously. He is very attached to his morning teacher so the questions start early, "Where is Kyky [his name for Kyla, the teacher]?" I make up answers for him depending on what time it is and what I figure her typical morning routine is. For instance, I might say, "Right now she's in the bathroom putting on her make-up and drying her hair."

Shortly after 8:00 a.m. his driver June picks him up to take him to school. She is a marvelous lady who has provided Josiah with consistent transportation over the past two and a half years. Each day we pray that she will arrive before the school bus picks up the other children. Josiah is very aware that he is different than other children and cries uncontrollably if he has to watch his brothers and the children from our daycare board the bus. His desire to ride the bus is so great that on weekends he will pretend to call the bus driver to come get him.

Josiah loves his school and is making great strides academically. When he's at home he frequently acts out parts of his school day. Josiah experiences significant anxiety at school and at home, so much of the time is spent making sure he is emotionally okay. Again his behavior ranges from one extreme to the other. He can have days of wonderful participation and gains and he can have other days where expectations have to be pulled back to the bare bones. Josiah still has to be physically restrained at times to keep him and others safe. However, he loves the other students as well as staff, and regularly impresses them with his memory for names and other information. He can be funny and sarcastic, which the staff find to be a real treat.

At 3:30 p.m. June picks Josiah up at school and brings him home. He always runs in the house to get a toy dinosaur, which he calls Little Foot, and then heads back out to find water to play in. He strips off any outerwear he may have been wearing in minutes, no matter what the weather is like outside. Apparently he does not experience cold like other people do. Running around in the yard, he excitedly anticipates the other children arriving home from school. He is a fury of activity from the time he steps in the door until he finally falls asleep.

CR

Anne and Alex (11)

The neurologist had been in the room with us for approximately ten minutes when she said, "Well, it's autism." I said, "That means—what? What do you do to treat this?" She replied, "I don't know what's available in your area. Go home and talk to your school district." That's all she told us. I remember staring at her while she was telling us this as I glanced at my child on the floor and thought, "What did she just say?" She offered nothing in the way of hope or a glimmer of anything that would make me feel okay about moving forward. When we came home and I talked to the school district they didn't seem to know what to do either. They offered to put him into a preschool program but provided little consolation or assurance that things would get better.

When we actually got Alex into the program, we were relieved because his preschool teacher was great. She made a lot of gains with him while he was under her care. In regard to his education since then, we have had a lot of issues with his speech therapy. Alex still has almost no verbal speaking skills. The school system here considers speech therapy getting a child to talk rather than working with them to communicate in any way. Alex has had many speech therapists and every one of them has had a different method of teaching things. There is almost no consistency in his program. Today they switched his speech and occupational therapists again, which makes the third time this year.

As Alex got older, we were encouraged by our local school system to send him to a major city where more specialized services were available for his education. This involves him traveling 50 miles by bus each school day. That is a long time to be on a bus and in the winter when he is in that vehicle and it is icy, every time I put him on the bus I'm putting his life in jeopardy.

It was agonizing to say, "Okay, we'll send him away," but we live in an iso-lated community where everyone knows everyone else so I don't dare go against what the school administrators want.

In Alex's case I believe the decision to send him outside the district was motivated by dollars and cents, and what was best for the school district, rather than providing what would truly benefit my child. When the idea first came up about sending Alex to the city school I told them, "You may be sending him, but he'll be home with us every night." I'm not about to allow my ten-year-old to leave home for good. Again, we live in a very small com-munity and we have to be very careful about what we say—we own our own business, and if you offend someone in a town like ours you can ruin your business. Sadly, with the amount of money they are paying the bus driver and for gas to transport him if they would just pay a personal assis-tant instead they'd probably end up ahead financially.

When Alex attended school in our town he was blessed with the abso-lute best classmates, who still love and adore him, and stop by the house to see him from time to time during the school year. For sixth graders to do that you know they have to be very special children. The lasting friendships Alex made stem from a wonderful kindergarten teacher who tried to make everything in the classroom something that he could participate in. She was also very good at explaining his disability to his classmates. Together she and I made a scrapbook with pictures of him and the other children, start-ing from when they were in preschool. There were pictures of his aides helping him do various things and we used it to show the kids what autism was and how things work with Alex. We started the book at the beginning of that year and I've kept adding to it each year. Now it is huge and filled with memories from when they were in kindergarten all the way up through the fifth grade. That book has been a great resource. When people ask things about Alex it's easy to pull the book out and say, "This might explain a little bit about it."

The whole special education process has been a real learning experi-ence for me. Coming from the perspective of an educator, I think you should do whatever you feel is best for the child, regardless of if the child is classified to receive special education services or not. However, from the time of our first encounter with "the IEP team" the reality was quite differ-ent from what I would have expected. After Alex was diagnosed we requested that the school district send somebody over to the daycare where he stayed after school to work with him. The principal said "the team" would talk about it, so I figured that must be one of the education teams I have heard so much about. I was so naive. I didn't even know who "the team" consisted of. Later that afternoon I received a telephone call to tell me that "the team" had decided it would not be in Alex's best interest to have someone work with him and that he needed some downtime in his schedule. We figured the deal was done and agreed.

On Sunday at church, sitting next to us was another family who has a daughter with Down's Syndrome. I was telling the mom what happened with our request and she said, "Weren't you guys at that meeting?" I said, "No, were we supposed to be?" and she said, "Oh! We need to educate you!" She informed me "the team" couldn't make the decision without our consent. We were supposed to be a part of the decision-making process. As I sit back and reflect on that situation, I think, why is it so difficult for the school districts to be open and honest with parents? All they had to do was explain that we were a part of the educational team and we make decisions together. How hard is that?

When Alex was first diagnosed, my husband and I decided, "We'll do this on our own. We're not going to ask anybody to do anything differently." I think our reasoning back then was to keep things as normal as possible. It *is* different though, and we quickly found out we needed help and that normal had to become a different kind of normal. I think this story a friend sent me explains it best:

Welcome To Holland
by
Emily Perl Kingsley

I am often asked to describe the experience of raising a child with a disability—to try to help people who have not shared that unique experience to understand it, to imagine how it would feel. It's like this...

When you're going to have a baby, it's like planning a fabulous vacation trip—to Italy. You buy a bunch of guide books and make your wonderful plans. The Coliseum. The Michelangelo David. The gondolas in Venice. You may learn some handy phrases in Italian. It's all very exciting.

After months of eager anticipation, the day finally arrives. You pack your bags and off you go. Several hours later, the plane lands. The stewardess comes in and says, "Welcome to Holland."

"*Holland?!?*" you say. "What do you mean Holland?? I signed up for Italy! I'm supposed to be in Italy. All my life I've dreamed of going to Italy."

But there's been a change in the flight plan. They've landed in Holland and there you must stay.

The important thing is that they haven't taken you to a horrible, disgusting, filthy place, full of pestilence, famine and disease. It's just a different place.

So you must go out and buy new guide books. And you must learn a whole new language. And you will meet a whole new group of people you would never have met.

It's just a *different* place. It's slower-paced than Italy, less flashy than Italy. But after you've been there for a while and you catch your breath, you look around…and you begin to notice that Holland has windmills…and Holland has tulips. Holland even has Rembrandts.

But everyone you know is busy coming and going from Italy…and they're all bragging about what a wonderful time they had there. And for the rest of your life, you will say, "Yes, that's where I was supposed to go. That's what I had planned."

And the pain of that will never, ever, ever, *ever* go away…because the loss of that dream is a very very significant loss.

But…if you spend your life mourning the fact that you didn't get to Italy, you may never be free to enjoy the very special, the very lovely things…about Holland.

I read that every once in a while when I get discouraged about something that happens with the schools and I need to remind myself that autism is my Holland—although sometimes it seems more like the Czech Republic!

CR

A professional's perspective: Judy, special education teacher

In 2001 I received my Master's degree in Special Education from Millersville University. As far as my professional academic preparation, most of it was not specific to children on the spectrum. I gained most of my experience in that area by substituting in a pilot program for children with autism. There was a child there that had profound autism and I learned a great deal working with him. My studies consisted of a variety of courses covering general special education issues, and some specific courses covering learning disabilities and mental retardation. Perhaps things have changed over the past five years, but I don't recall any one course that dealt specifically with autism or PDD. Autism was covered as a minor part of the course about moderate and profound emotional disturbances.

I decided to go back to school in my forties because my older son had some learning problems. He was diagnosed as gifted/learning disabled, and I believed I could help other children as I helped him. After my son had some academic difficulties I started volunteering to assist children with learning disabilities and behavior problems. I went to some classes provided by a local mental health organization and began tutoring children in my sons' classrooms and at a local private school. To my surprise, I found these experiences very gratifying and made the decision to pursue working with special needs children professionally.

My experience handling my son's challenges led me to seek out other children with special needs. All the difficult times I experienced with him taught me to be a better person and prepared me to deal with my chosen career. While I have been teaching only four years in my current position in the special education field, I worked as a substitute teacher for several years prior. Most of my time substituting was spent in the preschool special needs classes so I developed a real love for children in this age group.

The Intermediate Unit (IU) and school districts in Pennsylvania as well as the rest of the United States have experienced a dramatic increase in the number of students with Pervasive Developmental Disorder (PDD) over the past several years. We don't know exactly why, but we are finding more and more children in preschools with PDD. This IU has several preschool classes specifically designed for autistic support. In my class I have children with a variety of needs. This year I have one child labeled with autism, but there are several children with tendencies of PDD. In the past four to five years I have had only about three to four children with a diagnosis of autism in my classroom. However, we are seeing more and more children on the spectrum coming into our program.

Over the course of the school year I see major improvements in the children's skills and abilities. One of my strengths as a teacher is that I am very structured and consistent in what I do. I find children can't learn unless you have their attention, so I put an emphasis on positive and appropriate behavior. Having an organized classroom further increases a child's likelihood to pay attention. I have specific rules for behavior during structured and unstructured activities, including playtime. I use pictures to illustrate these rules and review them often with the children.

At our school we also use individual picture schedules and timers to aid in the transition between activities. This way there are no surprises, and the children always know what to expect. There are also color-coded foot-prints for them to stand on when they line up. These visual reminders really come in handy during a fire drill or similar change in routine where a speedy transition is necessary.

In reality, paperwork is the most challenging part of my job. The children are fairly easy, but the paperwork is endless. There are so many extra forms and documents to keep up with that it actually takes time away from the kids. Trying to get everything done seems impossible at times. Parents don't realize how much time I spend preparing for class and writing reports. I stay after school, take paperwork home at night, and spend Sunday afternoons preparing for the week.

Another challenging aspect of public education for me is that I can help the children in school but I can't do anything about their home lives. Many times, the successes I see at school are not being carried over at home. It is wonderful when parents and teachers can work together in order to obtain certain goals or behaviors. Family and parenting issues are some of the reasons why my IU has a program in which teachers visit the homes. Through these interactions, communication between parents and teachers is improved and they can work together to develop and implement strategies to help the child.

Perhaps the biggest reward of all is seeing the progress in the children and remembering how they were at the beginning of the year. Within a few months you can see some change in the child already and by the end of the year there are often dramatic results. In the course of a year I have had an opportunity to hear a child's first words and watch him make a friend for the first time. These are the most rewarding parts.

Sometimes the efforts of teachers can be misinterpreted. Parents might feel that teachers don't have their child's best interest at heart and some parents view teachers as adversaries. From my experience I believe the majority of teachers are very concerned with their students' welfare and try to support parents as much as possible. We may have to say things the parents don't want to hear or that are hard for them to accept. The things teachers say can be especially difficult for the parents of preschoolers to accept, as they are just being told that their child might have a certain disability. Parents may be in denial that anything is wrong. I know from personal experience that it can be difficult as a parent to go into an IEP meeting when there are ten other adults in there evaluating and making recommendations for your child. I have been through IEP meetings as a parent and sometimes questioned the outcome. You are part of the team—get involved and speak up!

As a parent, if you don't understand something or a certain aspect of your child's program isn't explained sufficiently it is easy to become upset. One way to address concerns right away is by using a communication log. I always encourage parents to come to me if they have a problem, and discuss any questions or concerns they might have. I make myself available at school and at home, and strive to keep the lines of communication open at all times.

The biggest thing I can tell parents is to communicate your expectations, needs, and desires. I cannot stress this enough. If the lines of communication are kept open and you approach the teacher in an open-minded, positive way everyone will benefit. As much as possible try to work together as a team; after all, it is in the best interest of the child. If you want to talk to the teachers, set up an email system, call them, or schedule an appointment. Most teachers are willing to establish a workable system of communication if requested by a parent.

As I mentioned before, I work with a variety of children with different levels of need. I see some of my children being very successful 20 years from now. Others may be involved in supervised employment or in the achievement of a personal goal. It is hard to project the future, but I have high hopes for all my students. I think positively and hope that each child will reach his or her potential.

Judy's tips

- Get as much information as you can—knowledge is power!

- Join support groups.

- Keep lines of communication with teachers and therapists open.

- Even if you question whether something is wrong with your child or not, get him checked out. The earlier the problem is identified, the earlier intervention begins and the greater the likelihood of success.

- Remember that every child on the spectrum is unique and different.

- Discover your child's strengths and needs in order to help him become more successful. Just because a child has a certain diagnosis doesn't mean he or she can't improve. Every child can become more successful depending on expectations for them and the kind of treatment they receive.

- Always try to keep a positive outlook and have the highest expectations that you can.

SOMETHING TO TALK ABOUT

1. What are the laws relating to special needs children? How can they benefit my child?

2. What recourse do I have if my child is not receiving services to which he is entitled?

3. How can I build a positive relationship with teachers and school administrators?

4. Why does it seem like I have to educate the teachers and school staff about autism? Shouldn't they already know about it?

5. Discuss the special education program in your area. Are there programs that you were not aware of that may benefit your child?

6. How should I go about educating my child's classmates about autism? What experiences have others had as they have visited their child's classroom?

7. How do I know if mainstreaming or a self-contained classroom is best for my child?

8. What are some of the major differences between public and private schools in the area?

9. How does the school district in my area interact with home-based therapy programs? Who should I contact in the area to learn more about these services?

REFLECTION ACTIVITY

Develop a 30-minute presentation to share with your child's classmates at school and make arrangements to present it within the next month. Involve your child as you deem appropriate. If you have already presented a similar program, find another parent in the same situation and share the format with them.

4.

Family Matters:
Marriage, Divorce,
and Everything in Between

Becca, Andy, Alex (4), and Josef (18 months)

Alex received the diagnosis of autism at 17 months. Currently Josef is diagnosed "at risk" and will probably be classified as Pervasive Developmental Disorder (PDD) or Asperger's when he gets a little older. Alex's verbal abilities are quite good now, but also consider that he has already had almost three years of intensive therapy. For both boys we used a home-grown, do-it-yourself, whatever works combination of Applied Behavioral Analysis (ABA), Floor Time, and dietary intervention, in addition to occupational therapy, music therapy, physical therapy, water therapy, hippotherapy (horses), gymnastics, and anything and everything that I thought might help break them out of their shells and get them to function. We received some funding to assist with the traditional therapies but everything else has been out of our pockets.

The financial aspects of living with autism can definitely put a strain on a relationship. During the first year alone my husband Andy and I spent $25,000 for medical costs. I remember filling out the tax papers and claiming it. I know there are tons more parents who take out second mortgages on their homes and home equity lines, and have tons of credit cards and go further into the hole with money every month. Those figures are for traditional therapies only—not taking into account all the diet and supplements and other therapies that aren't included. Everything is so expensive. But if there is a chance my kids will respond or if I see a change in their behavior you better believe I'll continue chipping in, whatever the cost.

Andy and I didn't have a whole lot of time together as a married couple before everything started happening with Alex. I'd already had two surgeries for endometriosis when I was younger, so we knew if we wanted a family we were going to have to try earlier rather than put it off. Thankfully we were successful. My pregnancies were very rough though—they were hard on me physically and I know it was difficult on Andy to come home and see me sick. We had just moved here to Arizona and hadn't had time to develop any close friendships yet. It was a tough time for both of us.

Our marriage went through a period where I wasn't sure we were going to be able to sustain it. The existing problems with Alex were compounded when Jo was born and there were obviously abnormal things going on with him. Jo actually has cerebral palsy on top of everything else. So we have another challenge that we are dealing with and we see a physical therapist for Jo's motor concerns. The stress level is high because Andy and I are always tired, but in a way it's made us stronger because we didn't give up on our kids or each other. We try to listen to each other even when we're so tired and grumpy that we can't even think of putting two words together to form a sentence.

For us, the biggest change occurred when Andy received the dual diagnosis of Asperger's and ADD. That explained a lot of the way he acted and it helped me to say, "I make allowances in my expectations for my kids and I need to make similar allowances in my expectations for my husband. I need to understand that he can't do certain things." I try to remember that it's difficult for Andy to do things like pay a bill on time or remember the three things I asked him to pick up at the grocery store. I need to give him a list. Having gotten through the first five years of marriage, dealing with both sets of our parents getting divorced and my stepfather passing away, and having two boys and a husband with developmental disabilities, I'd say we're doing okay. Things are better now and I'm confident about the future and that we'll be able to work through anything that comes our way.

Alex was on a waiting list for speech therapy for months after the diagnosis. There wasn't a time during that period where he wasn't getting constant speech therapy from me. We labeled absolutely everything. I would talk to him like he was a normal kid relentlessly, saying things like, "Alex, look at the green car. There's a blue car." We labeled everything. At dinner it was, "fries; hamburger; chicken; soup; beverage." When he finally started speaking I made him repeat the words.

Presently we're doing the same kinds of things with Josef. Josef didn't have any words at 15 months. Three months later he has the vocabulary of a two-and-a-half-year-old. It is constant work. I don't let any situation go without seeing a therapeutic benefit. I can turn almost anything into a teachable moment. There is not a situation where I can't find something for

Alex or Josef to learn from; I try to find what is appropriate for each child according to the level they are at. It's hard, but it's not rocket science.

At first there was a sacrifice that came with all that work. For the longest time my family and relatives, who lived far away, thought I was the coldest mother they knew. They'd make comments like, "You're so demanding from him. You're always expecting something from him. He needs to be a kid." I definitely had to put away some of my "mommy feelings" and maternal instincts. My kid would be crying because something was hard for him and I'd want to go over and hug him, but we kept working. Sure there are times when I've wanted to say, "It's okay if you go and stim, I won't make you work any more," but I don't. I know I don't have some of that connection other moms have with their kids because I am their teacher too. However, it's a trade-off that I'm comfortable making and I'd do it all again if I had to. Now that my relatives have seen the fruits of my labor, I don't get those types of comments any longer. The boys have responded well to therapy. My family understands now that I've done what I did because it made a difference.

My husband and I are in the process of adopting a third child and after much consideration we decided we don't want a normal, healthy baby. We are going to take a child that wouldn't survive otherwise. I don't know how to parent anything else. Other than raising these children, I believe my purpose in life is to help parents and families who are dealing with the strain of having a child with a disability. I have such a burden in my heart for the parents who lose their marriage over this. I don't feel that the support necessary exists for couples—there's nothing per se for husbands and wives. I want to work with families after they get the diagnosis and offer my services to counsel during those critical first two or three years after diagnosis because there are so many adjustment issues. Frequently one spouse may not understand what the other spouse is sacrificing or has to do during the day. Support for the marriage is crucial for a relationship to survive.

I've also noticed that I have had to give up some of that selfishness that is okay when you're not married and don't have children. We've had to learn when it's appropriate to take that time back and say, "We're going to take some time for us." More parents need to do that, not only for each other and themselves, but for the sake of their marriage. What a difference it makes when you say, "Tonight we're going to put the kids to bed early, we're going to turn the TV off, and we're going to sit here and light some candles and have dinner together. We're going to have some couple time." I'm not saying you have to actually go somewhere on a date, just be creative in your home if that's your only option or you can't get respite. Make time for each other and persist in all parts of the relationship, and let each other know that you're in this thing together.

In my life I've had a lot of unpleasant issues to deal with and I've found that it's easiest to make the best of whatever situation I'm in. Now that is not to imply that there aren't days when I struggle. There are those days when the kids watch way too much TV and they stim a lot more than they should. Some days when Andy gets home from work I tell him, "I'm done. I'm going upstairs and I'll see you tomorrow." From day to day it's sink or swim. The interventions we have tried have been very successful so that makes it easier—I can't imagine what it would be like to have a child who is unresponsive, regardless of how many therapy hours you put in. I'm sure it's a whole different ballgame for those parents.

We as parents have an awesome responsibility to raise and teach any child, whether he is a normal high school student who is a quarterback, cheerleader or president of the student body, or the profoundly deaf, blind child who had birth injuries. A lot of people would say, "Just give up on them," but I look at my job raising Alex and Josef as a gift rather than a burden. It's all a matter of perspective.

Becca's tip

- Make time for yourselves as a couple. Nourish your marriage—you need each other.

CR

Liz and Eric (14)

For Eric's sixth birthday instead of bringing presents we asked the extended family, including aunts, uncles, cousins, and grandparents, to give us some time. Everyone came over to our house for the party, and then we watched a variety of videos about autism. Because it was their gift to Eric people paid more attention. I could almost see light bulbs come on over their heads, even for the littlest kids. At last they realized Eric was not intentionally being mean when he hurt them, he just didn't understand how to act in certain situations. The best part was having my nieces and nephews (some who were as young as three years old at the time) finally understand that it was okay that Eric didn't have to share. They stopped thinking he was bad and accepted him.

From that point on everyone became more patient and tolerant with Eric. Taking an hour and a half to learn about autism made a huge impact on how our family viewed Eric, as well as a big difference in how my husband and I were perceived by our relatives. People weren't always trying to figure out what we were doing wrong or why our kid was so out of control. They had more patience with him, too. In a sense, it was a "re-birthday" for all of us.

CR

Maurine (grandmother) and Joshua (7)

My grandson, Joshua, is a child who has come a very long way since he was first diagnosed prior to his third birthday. He can be very loving and sweet at times. On the other hand he has always had a very aggressive side that is difficult to deal with. Joshua's tantrums have diminished from when he was young, although he still has them. Temperamentally there are two extremes of Joshua's behavior, as there are with many autistic children.

As far as assistance from other family members we are really limited because of where we live, in South Carolina. Joshua hasn't had any contact with his father in two years and my ex-husband died of lung cancer this past January, so Joshua and his brother lost their grandfather, too. They've never met their other grandparents. I have three sisters, but they live at opposite ends of the country, so we seldom see them. For me, it would make things a lot easier if they were closer and the kids would really benefit from having family nearby.

Next door to us lives an older gentleman, Marion, who is a retired English teacher. He has taken it upon himself to work with Joshua and become his special friend. Marion takes him for walks and doesn't mind spending time with him. Joshua has really taken to him. Even when Joshua's grandfather was alive, he wasn't too sure how to deal with him so until Marion came into the picture Joshua never really had a father figure. Luckily this neighbor has taken the responsibility upon himself to help nurture the children and they love him as much as they would any blood relation. If I walk outside and Joshua is with Marion he says, "Go home, Grandma, I want to be with Marion and I'm not sharing him."

Autism has been my life for five years. My daughter sort of burnt out after the first year and has left a majority of Joshua's care up to me. I take care of his medicines, therapy, and all the biomedical treatments. She doesn't get involved. I guess I don't blame her, she is only 30 years old, she's still young and she wants to get married again. She likes to go out and be with her friends, so in essence I've been the mom.

I give the boys 100 percent of my energy. My reward is watching Joshua improve and seeing both boys grow up healthy and strong. Joshua has come a tremendously long way and I'll be there for him every step of the way.

Autism is exhausting. I don't have a lot of time for myself. My sisters and my mother keep telling me to make time for myself, that I've got to have my own life outside of the kids, but I not sure when they expect that to happen. Everyone seems to think I have a choice, but personally I don't feel ensuring Joshua has what he needs is optional. Choice or not, this is the direction I am supposed to take right now. Perhaps some day, before I'm too old, I'll have some time to do things I enjoy again. Right now there's not enough time in the day.

Maurine's tip

- Remember, there is hope! I know parents who have autistic children who are now in normal classrooms and you cannot tell them from the other kids.

CR

Nancy (grandmother) and Christina (6)

Christina is my beautiful granddaughter. She is a very outgoing child except when she gets upset. When she gets excited she flaps her arms. She talks to anyone that she comes into contact with and has no fear of strangers. She also likes to run so she must be watched every second as I'm sure she could get lost very quickly.

I had thought something was wrong with Chrissy for a while; I just wasn't in the position to do anything about it. Around the time she turned one and a half years old, she started flapping her arms and stopped looking directly at people. Her parents had her tested and the doctors said that she had Pervasive Developmental Disorder-Not Otherwise Specified (PDD-NOS), but they didn't recommend any type of therapy for her at that time. Chrissy didn't come to live with us permanently until she was a year old.

When the state made me Chrissy's legal guardian, I took her to see a developmental pediatrician. He diagnosed her as having ADHD as well as a behavior disturbance and obsessive-compulsive behaviors. He prescribed her the medication Ritalin and then later tried her on Adderall. There were negative side effects with both medications so we discontinued them. The school categorized her learning problems as "communicative impaired."

Through all this, I still felt there was something else wrong with Chrissy. She was having a very hard time in school and not adjusting well at all. The teachers tended to isolate her from the other children, and implied that they thought she was lazy. I decided to get a complete evaluation on Chrissy by an autism expert. I thought she just had the PDD-NOS, but he said that she does not have ADHD or PDD, but the actual diagnosis of autism. I suspected something and wasn't too surprised; however, to actually hear the word "autism" applied to Chrissy did upset me. Now, after talking with many parents I realize that it may be for the best to have the autism label. She will qualify for the school and special support that she so desperately needs. I am in the process of trying to get physical therapy and occupational therapy for her. We are still fighting for these and other services.

Raising any child would be a challenge at my age, but I simply do what I have to for Chrissy's sake. Her grandfather and I accept her for who she is and love her regardless of her condition. I hope and pray Chrissy will be able to be self-sufficient someday and perhaps hold a good job. She is so sweet and special, and I feel with lots of love and support it will happen. I am 61 years old now and just want to live long enough to see her graduate from high school. I do fear what will happen to Chrissy should something happen to my husband and me. What will the future hold for her without us? Only time will tell.

Today, Chrissy is doing quite well and I believe she will do even better with additional therapy. Autism is what makes her Chrissy. No one is perfect—this is who she is. My Chrissy is very loving and has lots of hugs to give. I think my life with Chrissy has changed me for the better. I must admit that Chrissy takes a lot of my time and energy. Life used to be a lot easier before she came to live with us. On the other hand, I love her very much and she is very loving in return. I would not change a thing about our situation because Chrissy is my world and I would never give her up!

Nancy's tips

- Never give up.
- Show your child all the love and support she or he deserves.
- Be aggressive on behalf of your child and learn to fight for what they need.

CR

Richard and Sarah (12)

Sarah was diagnosed with PDD at 18 months. Most of my time spent with her is on the weekends, as I work during the week. Her days during the week are a blur to me because I don't get home until late, so the weekends are for us. Saturday morning Sarah gets up, watches television, has breakfast, and then I take her to a piano lesson.

We knew something was wrong with Sarah from an early age. She was the easiest child to take care of, whereas her older sister Danielle was a bit more of a challenge. My wife, Debbie and I both worked and we would take the girls to a babysitter during the day. Danielle would constantly look for attention but Sarah for the most part would be content watching TV, rocking, or playing with a toy, needing little or no interaction from others. The babysitter would say things like, "Sarah was such a doll, we put her on the floor and she just played with the belt all day. She is so cute." We thought, "Okay, cute…but odd," so we decided to take her to the pediatrician because there was something that just didn't seem to click.

When you have two children close together it's easy to focus on the one looking for attention. But with Sarah we did begin to wonder if something was really wrong or if we were just being bad parents. We started telling the doctors that there was something wrong, but that we weren't sure what it was, so we were given an appointment to see a specialist. After completing the battery of tests, we were told our daughter was autistic. We expected to hear, "Pay more attention to your child," we certainly were not prepared to hear that!

Just prior to the diagnosis we had taken out a second mortgage on our home and were in the middle of renovating it. A short while later I was informed my job was going to be outsourced to another company. Suddenly there we were: a young family, remodeling our home, in debt up to our eyeballs, with me getting ready to lose my job and, to top it all off, I have an autistic child. In a matter of months it seemed like our world had completely fallen apart. On the bright side, we have had a lot of family support. The grandparents were involved from the start and have been there for us ever since.

I know there are a lot of fathers out there doing wonderful things for children, but it seems that a majority of the parents I meet online, at autism conferences, or at meetings are moms. A substantial number of them are single parents. I don't understand why this is, but I definitely think the women outnumber the men in this fight and the fathers need to take action. As parents we need to share the burden and work together to help the children rather than wasting precious energy blaming each other for the situation or feeling guilty that we caused the autism.

When I look back in time I realize finding out that Sarah had autism at 18 months of age was not such a bad thing. The doctor was able to get us connected with Early Intervention and we met some super people through them. One of the people I met directed me to a fathers' group and attending the group reassured me I was not alone. Meeting other fathers who were dealing with similar struggles and making friends in the same boat made it easier for me personally to deal with the situation and to come to terms with the challenges I would be facing in the future. Having the support of other fathers provided a different perspective, and enabled me to face this new challenge and refocus on my entire family, not just autism.

My wife and I always wonder if we are doing right by our children, especially when we see things like segments on television or read stories about families giving up their lives to save their children. An article will tell you about a woman who gave up her career to work full-time with her child or how they travel all over the world for treatments of the new miracle cure. I want to tell parents to not believe everything they hear. In the real world, I have to work, put food on the table, pay my bills, and support my family in general. I can't just stop living and quit my job to make things right. Besides, we have more than one child so if we focused too much on autism our other child would probably get lost in the process.

Although I would never wish autism on anyone, I will say that my life has been enriched by Sarah's uniqueness. She teaches us unconditional love, blind trust, and simply joy. The trials we face with her are small compared to the challenges other families face dealing with other disabilities. If you asked me how my life has changed now that I have a daughter with autism, my answer would be that my life changed because I had a daughter not because I had a daughter with autism. As a parent if your life is not constantly changing, you need to spend more time at home.

Richard's tips

- If you wouldn't do it to my child don't do it to yours.
- Don't believe everything you hear.
- You're the parent—don't second-guess your decisions.

☙

Jamie, Scott, and Sarah (6)

I look at everything in terms of BA (Before Autism) and AA (After Autism). Life is completely different now that we have a child with special needs. All the patterns and traditions in our family have changed. Our marriage is strained. Scott and I have 15 years of marriage and four kids together, and nothing has ever come between us but this.

In our situation, I am the one primarily responsible for caring for Sarah. Even though it was my decision, I admit that I was resentful of carrying that burden alone. My husband wasn't at fault, but I blamed him anyway. While he knows the basics of what's going on with Sarah's therapy, he's at work all day so isn't able to be too hands on. The first few years after Sarah was diagnosed were really rough on us. I was so full of emotion I wasn't thinking straight. We were separated for a while, but we are working things out. Making any permanent decisions about our marriage during that time would have been a big mistake.

Autism is a long road. For us, it's probably something we'll be dealing with in one form or another for the rest of our lives. Quite possibly Sarah will be dependent on us until we die, so I think it's best that we decided to stay together. Although Sarah's behaviors aren't going to magically stop because we've decided to work together, I believe when you are sharing the burden it can make your marriage stronger rather than tearing it apart.

Dealing with everything related to Sarah's disorder put me over the edge emotionally. Recently I was diagnosed with Bipolar Disorder. I've read that for some people Bipolar Disorder is triggered by trauma, and autism is my trauma. God's been with me through it all, though, and thankfully I'm okay. I am able to continue to work for Sarah and she needs me 100 percent right now. Luckily when I wasn't doing so well I had a great team working for Sarah. Everything was in place and held together, despite my inability to contribute.

Also, things have changed for our other children since Sarah's treatment started. My son Kyle (14) went from being an honor role student to getting straight Fs. As a teenager he definitely senses the tension we are under at home. He is the oldest and is fully aware of the way things used to be. He knew what a normal life was, so he misses it. My other girls, Courtney (10) and Ashley (7), don't really remember what life was like before all the doctor appointments and therapy began, so they handle it a little better.

Jamie's tips

- Use your anger and other emotions to motivate you to help your child.

- Stay dedicated, aware, and involved, making sure the child continually uses what they are learning.

ᏟᎡ

Jean and Jimmy (16)

After Jimmy's diagnosis, my husband became distant and preoccupied with work. He would let me handle all the doctor appointments and Individualized Education Program (IEP) meetings, in addition to the general care of Jimmy and my other sons. Financially, we couldn't afford for him to take time off from work, therefore I was left to attend to everything by myself. There was no extra money for him to attend conferences and seminars even if he had wanted to. I felt like I was doing everything alone. The child care, cooking, cleaning, and all other household responsibilities were completely left to me. This went on for many years and my resentment toward what I considered my absentee partner grew bigger and bigger.

Two years ago I finally decided I couldn't take it any more. I was at the lowest point in life; all the burdens had taken their toll on me. On Valentine's Day, I sat down and wrote a long letter to my family apologizing for what I was going to do. By taking most of the medications that were stacked up on our kitchen counter I tried to commit suicide. Fortunately, my husband found me before the attempt was complete.

Since then he has been a model husband. He helps with the chores even after a long day at work. He also takes an active interest in what is going on with Jimmy's school, doctor appointments, and our children's lives in general. I guess neither of us realized how strong he could be until it was almost too late. Unfortunately, I reached a point where I felt so low there seemed to be no other way out and death was the only option I saw to alleviate the pressures placed upon me.

Jean's tip

- Seek counseling if things seem so terrible that you don't want to go on.

ᏟᎡ

Karen and Dylan (7)

Since the kids' grandparents don't live in the same town, my husband and I lean heavily on each other for support. Our marriage is stronger because of all we've been through together, but I'm sure it didn't hurt that we'd been married 12 years before Dylan was born. For certain, we were better equipped to handle things than a young married couple dealing with a firstborn. We kid about that sometimes and say, "Well you know if Dylan had been Logan we probably would have ended up divorced!" We had only been married a couple of years when our older son was born. When you have a child when you are first married it is hard enough anyway. If we had a child with special needs when we were newly married, I doubt if our marriage would have survived. Having a child changes everything anyway, but a special needs child just adds to the confusion.

After 12 years of togetherness we were settled in our ways as a couple and had gotten used to being parents. That's not to say it wasn't hard and there weren't some trials, but we've managed to keep it together. The biggest lesson we've learned is that our needs and wants don't come first any more. It's challenging because my husband works an average of 60 hours per week so I can be the one constant for Dylan. With that arrangement we aren't always having to compromise about whose turn it is to take care of Dylan. Even though there are times I want to scream because it's so frustrating, for us that's just the way it has to be.

Our family is on an emotional rollercoaster most of the time: Mom's tired, cranky, and worn out; Dad's stressed out because he's always working; and Logan (15) just wants to make it all better. Logan has been my easy child and has never given me any trouble, but it upsets me that he had to grow up so quick. It's like he's 15 going on 30 because he's so afraid of causing problems for us.

Regardless of our emotional state, my husband and I view every step forward as a milestone. We don't look at what Dylan can't do—instead we say, "Look at everything he can do!" Admittedly, he's not your typical seven-year-old but now the doctors are telling us he's only two years behind, so we're making strides. Ten or fifteen years ago most people would have told us to put him in an institution and forget about him. Today, there are all these treatments and therapies, and kids can make substantial gains. For us we choose to keep moving ahead, even if we take baby steps. We take what Dylan gives us and go with it.

Karen's tip

- Remember, hope is the one thing no one can take from you.

❧

Kristen, Ed, and Jack (8)

Kristen says: Jack is really busy, very active, and has a great sense of humor. He doesn't sit still long. He does have some language, but when he does talk, it's not always appropriate. He loves playing outside. During the year he attends public school where he's mainstreamed with an aide. On a typical day, we walk him to the classroom in the morning and one of us picks him up at the end of the day on the way home. Sometimes a therapist comes to our home after school or we might take him to do Relationship Development Intervention (RDI) with an autism specialist through the school district. When we're not busy with an appointment Jack loves to go swimming. His grandparents have a swimming pool that we can use year round so we do that quite a bit.

When people ask, "How are you doing?" and "How is he doing?" it is difficult to give them an answer. I end up trying to explain to people that life is a different kind of normal, because I don't know what a "normal" life would be like. I can't just pick up and go to the grocery store or do something spontaneous any more. With Jack I always have to be thinking one step ahead and tell him what is coming next. How do you explain to someone that if you turn down the wrong street or go to the wrong store everything goes into crisis mode? You adjust, and after a while you become accustomed to a different type of normal. Sometimes I look at other people's lives and think, "Oh, wouldn't it be nice if we could do that?" The grass is always greener on the other side of the fence. I'm sure they have problems too, but sometimes I think it'd be nice to go to little league games or all the things I expected to do with a son. I can do that with my daughter, but it's still different.

Research shows that the stress of parenting kids with special needs contributes to marriages ending in divorce. I think for us it had the opposite effect: it brought us closer as a couple. Neither one of us was willing to do it on our own so we knew we were in it together. Caring for Jack definitely puts extra tension on his father, especially considering he wants to spend most of the time with his dad. Jack is very demanding on Ed; always wanting his full attention. I know it is exhausting. When my husband's gone,

I'm an acceptable substitute but when Dad's here he wants him and him only. He's just a one-person kid.

Ed says: Every aspect of our life is different since Jack was diagnosed. It's hard to say how our life has changed due to autism because he was our first child. Life was bound to change regardless of his condition, just maybe not so drastically. We had him diagnosed so early I almost can't even remember what normalcy was. This is the only way of life we have known for six-plus years.

The biggest thing that people don't understand is not being able to do normal family things like go to dinner at a restaurant, go to the store, or a baseball game. We always have to factor in where we are going, what that environment is going to be like, and Jack's ability to tolerate it. We usually can't go to a restaurant and sit there long enough to make it through ordering the meal, eating, and waiting to pay. Jack doesn't work that way. For instance, we might sit down and order food and then Jack is ready to go, so we go.

In every little aspect of daily life, we are always thinking ahead: "What do we have to worry about with this situation? Should we take two cars in case I need to leave with Jack and you need to stay?" Every holiday function we go to my wife and daughter go together in one car and Jack and I go in the other because we know he'll never last the six hours for Thanksgiving dinner at somebody's house. The same is true with Christmas. Little things like that are everyday things, but we've got to anticipate a different outcome. Whether it's grocery shopping or what seems like the most basic activity, we always wonder, "Is Jack going to be able to do okay?"

In my experience I've found that it's easy to be angry and upset, and want to blame something or somebody, but being mad doesn't fix anything. At some point I realized the quicker I was able to accept it, get over it, buy into it and start looking at how to make the situation better, the better things were going to be. There are a million different therapies, but the biggest key is just getting on with it. The hard part is to accept what cards you got dealt, and try and make the best hand you can. There were plenty of days when I could have sat around and cried and felt sorry for myself, but I knew that wouldn't make anything better for Jack. Every father dreams of taking his boy to little league and soccer practice, and things like that, but for me that isn't going to happen; I just have to accept that and move on.

Sometimes it's easy for me to get bogged down day to day because I always want Jack to be doing better than he is. One day he'll make a gain in one area and the next day he'll regress in some other aspect. It is a constant fight to continue moving forward. It seems there is always something to deal with or some aspect of Jack's life I'm puzzling over and it can weigh me down. I do that all the time. I'm constantly feeling like we should be doing something better.

However, when I stop for a moment and look at the big picture and see where we were three years ago, I am amazed at how far Jack has actually come. He's doing great. He's talking so clearly. Those are the things you kind of have to step back and catch when you pop in a video tape and look back at when they were first diagnosed. When you take a wider perspective, progress becomes clear.

Personally, I sometimes live Monday to Friday just so I can recoup on the weekends. Kristen and I are lucky in that we offset each other pretty well. She deals with certain things better and I deal with other things better. Jack obviously wants me more, like she said, but she does a great job of keeping me from getting totally taxed out. Divorce rates are high and we have met single parents locally (a few of them have actually gotten remarried to each other) but I honestly have no idea how they get by. I feel like we're getting our butts kicked with our set-up so I don't know how people cope alone.

Another frustrating part of autism for me is that the kids are never the same, so what works for mine doesn't always work for yours, and vice versa. There are all these commonalities and similar symptoms and yet they all respond so differently to each type of treatment. What helps one child off the charts does nothing for mine. I can't stand it when you go to a conference and you learn about something new and you say, "Oh God, maybe this will really do it!" and then you invest all this time and this money and absolutely nothing happens. That's one of those things you learn to accept. It was harder when we were young and just starting out; we kept hoping the next thing we tried would be the magic bullet. Now I understand in many cases it's a matter of cumulative treatments that you continue to build upon and you just have to persevere without seeing a lot of results all at once. You want them to take a pill and make it go away but what is really necessary is just getting in there and working. Everything is so hands on and intensive. There's nothing easy about any of it.

Kristen and Ed's tips

- Jump in and get going.
- Change your expectations if necessary.
- Start with the most basic things first and give your child a strong foundation for future learning. Build on what they can handle.

○℞

Stacy, Ryan and Brenna (10)

It is nice to see things from a man's point of view. One day I picked up a book, *Breaking Autism's Barriers: A Father's Story*, that Ryan left lying around while he was at work and noticed he had highlighted sentences and paragraphs. He even had notes in the margins in the book. Later when I met the author, Bill Davis, at a book signing he flipped through the copy noticing all the highlighted pages. We talked for a while about the challenges that fathers experience. It was refreshing to speak to a man who understood. I only wish Ryan could have been there to meet him in person.

Our marriage has had its ups and downs. Autism is very stressful on the child, the siblings, the parents, and the family in general. I am calmer than Ryan, but I also understand he has a very stressful job. Therefore when he gets home, he just likes to sit and relax. Unfortunately that just doesn't happen around here until bedtime.

❧

Susanne, Hans, and Sam (11)

It was a crisp autumn night and I was going on a blind date set up by well-meaning friends. The guy was from Belgium so at least I wouldn't have to worry about it becoming anything serious, he wasn't planning to stay in America. At 26, the thought of marriage was pretty well out of my head; I had my job, two cats, and savings for an early retirement. I wanted children but figured if I couldn't have my own, I could always borrow one of my nieces or nephews. Despite a large difference in our ages and the contrived beginning, Hans and I formed a fast friendship. We enjoyed just being together, talking and laughing. This went on for a year and then it was time for him to return home. On Hans's last night in America our friends threw a going-away party; both of us had a bit too much to drink and one thing led to another...

A few weeks later I started feeling very nauseated and it kept getting worse. Shortly thereafter it struck me: *I was pregnant!* How could I have let this happen? Single mom, no job, no insurance, and the father thousands of miles away. I was alone and there wasn't anyone I could turn to. My friends who had introduced us were of little help, with one saying she'd adopt the baby and the other saying I should force Hans to be part of the whole thing.

"He's only 19, in another country, and not ready for a family," I argued. It was then I decided it would be better for all if I just kept my mouth shut.

The one friend that had wanted to adopt my baby became angry when I refused to give it up for adoption; that was the last I saw of her. The other friend, Jackie, just sighed and told me she didn't agree with my decision to go on with the pregnancy alone but would honor my wishes.

Sam was born on a cold April night after 48 hours of labor and an emergency C-section. He was 7.5 lbs, 22.75 inches long, with black hair, and had the biggest gray eyes framed by the longest, thickest lashes. His hair would later turn blondish-brown and his eyes a deep coffee brown. I joked that he looked like the baby monkeys you see on the Discovery Channel, but he was really precious. He was mine.

From the beginning Sam had colic and screamed night and day. The only time he was able to rest was when I drove to the ends of the earth in my car. It wasn't until I found "mommy bear" that he finally found some peace. He would snuggle the soft fur and listen to the "whoosh whoosh" sounds she emitted, wrapped in his blanket, rubbing the silky band that ran around it between his little fingers and thumb. I would hold him and rock him, watching him sleep.

Sam walked and talked early, and was even partly potty trained at one year. Then, bit by bit, he stopped talking and went back to wearing diapers full-time. I asked the pediatrician if this was normal and he reassured me that this sometimes happened and it is nothing to worry about, he'd get it back. It would take working with him for a year before he gained back his speech. I was forcing him to say words that he had said easily before such as "drink" and "eat." He was four years old before he was fully potty trained. Sam was anything but graceful; always tripping over his own feet, with bruises from falling and bumping into things. He never seemed to grasp abstract ideas and would often drift into his own little world. Little things would bother him and he'd break down in tears. Still the doctor said he was normal, just a little behind.

Juggling work and motherhood was harder than I had thought it would be. The time came when my savings were exhausted and I had to find a job. I really didn't want to leave Sam, but he was going to start nursery school so he wouldn't miss me with new friends to play with. He was okay, but the teacher said that he preferred his own company and often daydreamed.

Then came the time for regular school. Sam was four years old. He was so excited, wanting to make friends and proud that he was a big guy now. By the end of the first week, his enthusiasm had waned; by the end of the second week, he would hide his shoes or anything to delay going; by the end of the third week he would go into what I know now is a meltdown. It took everything I had to get him to school.

I decided to talk to the teacher. "Sam has ADHD," she said. "He needs to go to our doctor for a prescription for Ritalin." So I asked her, "What makes you think he has ADHD?" "He doesn't pay attention or follow directions." I asked, "Does he interrupt class? Is he hyperactive? What are you basing this diagnosis on?" She stated, "No, but…" I took him to our family doctor, he did an assessment and I was told Sam didn't have ADHD: he was a dreamer walking to the beat of a different drum. The school continued to insist that I put Sam on Ritalin but I wasn't about to give him medicine he didn't need. At this stalemate they told me, "Either you put him on it or he can't attend our school." I began homeschooling him shortly thereafter.

Life quickly became an endless circle of working and Sam. I just didn't have the time for anything or anyone else. Then my friend Jackie, who had stood by me when I was pregnant, came back into my life. She was amazed at my challenges with Sam and told me that I should have let Hans know.

Through my friend's well-intentioned meddling and a series of unforeseeable events she arranged for Hans to call (another "blind date" so to speak). That night I sat for the longest time, looking at the phone. Sam was back from his playgroup and I decided no lessons; it was just too much to cope with this looming over my head. Three hours passed, I made dinner for Sam, but my stomach was in knots. Then it was Sam's bedtime, so I gave him a bath and told him a story.

An hour later the phone rang. My insides were shaking; my hands were trembling so bad it was as if I was suddenly ice cold. Three rings, I reached for the phone and answered in a shaking voice: "Hello?"

"Hi, this is Hans. I hope you don't mind, Jackie gave me your number?" With my voice soft, and fear and uncertainty in my heart, I answered, "I doubt you remember me, it's Susanne."

"Oh my God! You're joking?" he sounded surprised. There was a silence and then he asked what I had been up to. It was now or never, I thought. "Well I'm working and taking care of my son," I mentioned. "You have a son," he asked. "How old? I didn't know you got married; you're not still are you?" "No. I never got married. Yes. I have a son; his name is Sam, and he is five." "Wow, who's the father? Does he have anything to do with him?"

This was just too much. Inside I was laughing and crying at the same time. All I could say was, "No, he hasn't had anything to do with us. I never told him. I couldn't force him into fatherhood when it was a drunken mistake." Silence. Did he understand what I was saying? I asked him, "Are you married?"

"No, I haven't met anyone here," he stated. "I'm going to be back in the States soon. Would it be okay if we got together?" It was then it hit me that I had to tell Hans the truth. "I'd like that but, before we do, you need to know that Sam is yours. I understand if you don't want to see us." I just told the father of my son that he's a dad over the phone after all these years! After a moment Hans said he'd arrange for an early vacation and would be there this weekend to talk.

When Hans arrived off the airplane we stood there for a minute just looking at each other. My knees felt like jelly. Then he walked forward and gave me a hug and said, "I am sorry. You should have told me." With those words, I knew things were going to be all right. We went to the only restaurant that was open in the wee hours and sat talking. I told him about Sam, showing him baby pictures and catching up on other things. When I stopped my babbling he said, "Marry me?"

"*What!* I don't want to get married to someone because they feel they have…" He interrupted and said, "I want to marry you because from the first time we met I knew you were the one; I was just too stupid to admit it then. You're smart, funny, not bad to look at, and all I ever wanted. The fact that we have a son is just an added bonus." I looked at him and decided: *Yes.*

We went to the registrar's office that Monday and filed for our marriage license. We were married that Friday.

Sam and I decided to reside in Belgium since he had the better job and had family that he didn't want to move away from. The law in Belgium requires all children that are of school age to attend. Unless you're rich and can afford a private international school you're stuck with their system. I wanted Sam to have language classes first, but they refused to wait, saying he would learn at school. He will either sink or swim; we'll see how it goes.

We took him in for testing and it was decided he would start with a year younger than his grade since he would be familiar with the material and that would make it easier for him to pick up the language. According to all the tests they ran he was above average and had normal intelligence. I tried to explain a bit about what went on with his education before, but they told me that they were the professionals.

The first two years went okay; the only major complaint from his teachers was that Sam had to be reminded to do things. The second year he would see his first little sister born. Then the third year everything went wrong. It was the first year of his school in the States x 100. Sam begged us to not make him go to school; every day was a struggle. I felt him slipping away. He didn't want anyone near him. Each day he became more withdrawn and the meltdowns grew stronger and lasted longer; he became almost unrecognizable from the sweet boy he had been the year before.

Frustrated and searching for answers, Hans took a day off and went to the school. When he came home the look on his face told me it wasn't going to be good news. After a glass of pop, he informed me that behind our backs the teacher and school had contacted the Board of Education requesting Sam be evaluated to see a psychologist. He had an appointment in a week. Sam was failing.

At the doctor's office she sat behind her desk looking at the folder she had on Sam; she never looked at him or talked to him. She then looked up at us and said, "After reviewing this file I'd say Sam probably has ADHD. Here is a prescription for Ritalin. If he doesn't respond well to that use this other script for Risperdal." My heart stopped and then I burst out, "How can you say what he has or doesn't have without even talking to him or even doing an exam?" She looked at me and said, "I'm going by what this file says." I refused to medicate our son without a proper exam.

Instead of unifying us, Hans and I were being torn apart by the stress. Things got worse as our youngest child doesn't sleep much, and Hans and I were barely talking. In the meantime, the school had Sam tested and gave us the results: Sam was mentally retarded. He was unable to do the work in his grade and had probably advanced as far as he could in a traditional setting. They recommended that we send him to a special school. My jaw hit the floor and then my temper flared, "How does a child go from being normal intelligence, top of his class, to the bottom and mentally retarded in one year?"

Reviewing the test questions, I noticed that all the things covered were things he knew how to do; he just refused to do them. It wasn't that he couldn't do them, he just wouldn't. "He knows this stuff! What happened when you gave him this test?" I implored. The school official stated, "We found that Sam couldn't do the work. This decision is final." That was it. No discussion.

We left the meeting bewildered, neither of us talking, just leaning on each other for support. What was there to say? Hans arranged three days off from work and set up appointments at the various special schools. We had no real choice, it was either one of these schools or Sam and I returning to the States so he could be homeschooled again. I stayed up that night searching the Internet for information on learning disabilities. It was time I opened my eyes and saw what was really wrong with my Sam.

After a few hours, I found a website for Asperger's Syndrome and, as I went down the list, more and more boxes were checked off. Now I had to face the fact my little boy wasn't being lazy, stubborn, and spoiled rotten, but that he may actually fall on the autistic spectrum. I stared at the screen, tears rolling down my face, feeling as if I had failed him. I searched madly for any and all information available. The more I found, the more pieces of the puzzle were filled in. It was a relief to finally have some clues, but at the same time I just wanted Sam to be okay.

The next morning I showed Hans all I had found. I had printed out everything I could until the printer ran out of ink and showed him the checklist. He went down each item and sat back in shock. While Sam didn't fit the criteria perfectly, Hans recognized a lot of his traits in the description.

During the first month of Sam's new school they did a complete evaluation, talked with him, and they got to know one another. After the tests were completed we were called in for a meeting. It was a moment of dread and anticipation.

"We've completed our tests, and despite what the Board says, Sam is far from being mentally retarded. He's actually quite bright. We have also found that he does show some symptoms of Asperger's and he has learned to cope remarkably well. Unless you know what to look for it is quite possible to miss." My heart sank. "We feel that, with help, Sam may be able to go on to attend university if he wants and works hard. While he has learned to cope, he is going to be entering puberty soon and it will be harder for him unless we can give him the tools to cope." It was a very encouraging discussion. The school recommended that he receive counseling and some one-on-one instruction, but no medication would be necessary. Because of this late diagnosis they also recommended counseling for us.

Sam loves his new school. He feels safe and accepted, which has been remarkable for his progress. The meltdowns are almost completely gone and the future is looking brighter. It is my hope that he will continue to improve and be able to live as normal a life as possible.

As for Hans and me, we are working on our relationship—one day at a time. Hans has learned that he needs to quit taking things for granted and I'm learning I can't carry the load by myself. It's hard for both of us since Hans is gone 12 hours a day with a full-time job and attending college in the evenings. We have switched off the auto-pilot, though, and are working together not to crash. We now arrange time for us to get away so that we can recapture what we almost lost and listen to each other. I don't know if we will make it, but it won't be because we didn't try.

The new school has helped by getting parents together to support each other. We have set up a network to give each other much needed breaks and play dates for our children. Life isn't all rosy but we have learned that we aren't alone. Instead of being lost in the system, Sam now has a chance. What could have destroyed our relationship has made us see that we have something worth fighting for. I hope the best for all children like Sam and that some day the rest of the world will be able to understand our children that walk to the beat of a different drum.

Susanne's tips

- Take it a day at a time. Don't bottle up your emotions until you explode—a good cry is okay!

- Find the humor where you can. Laughter can be a great release.

- Learn to accept what is, but never settle for what can change. If no one listens at first, keep at it until you get their attention.

- Talk to other parents.

- Read all you can.

- If there are no support groups try to set one up with other parents in the same boat, or visit online groups—sometimes, just knowing someone else out there understands can be a big help.

CR

A professional's perspective: Cary Pope, M.S., Doctoral Student, Department of Counselling and Human Development Services, The University of Georgia

Receiving the diagnosis of autism is clearly a major life event, which causes significant stress on the parents. The lifetime of care that parents can expect to provide is overwhelming. The reality of the child's limited life, the loss of expectations for the child the parents hoped to have, and the burden of care for the child affect the parents.

As a third-year doctoral student in Counseling Psychology at the University of Georgia, my training has included intensive couples and marital counseling. Based on my experience in working with parents of children with Autism Spectrum Disorders, certain themes have arisen across couples that appear to strongly impact the level of marital stress. For example, many parents of children with autism experience depression, anxiety, and hopelessness, and feel a lack of support from their spouse, friends, and family. Research indicates that parents move through a four-stage process in adjusting and adapting to the diagnosis of autism. The pre-diagnosis stage is characterized by the onset of parental observations of behavioral signs of the presence of an Autism Spectrum Disorder. This stage involves confusion regarding the cause of the behavior, feelings of self-blame, and severe stresses on family relationships. In addition, parents may experience frustration related to delay of services leading to an appropriate diagnosis. During this waiting period, parents may be given false reassurances, or even a false diagnosis.

In the diagnosis stage, parents appear to exhibit mixed emotions. Many parents are relieved to finally put a label to their child's unusual behavior, and the diagnosis enables them to access available support networks. However, many parents experience shock and disbelief when receiving the initial diagnosis. They may even reject the diagnosis. They may suffer a sense of trepidation, disbelief, and depression upon receiving the diagnosis of autism. Often parents blame themselves for the diagnosis. Many parents lack sufficient time to take care of themselves, feel socially isolated, and ineffective, and therefore need emotional support at this stage.

In the post-diagnosis stage parents are faced with a wide range of concerns. Adapting to the diagnosis has been compared to a process of grieving for the "hoped for" child. Parents will probably feel grief for the "expected" child they lost, and feelings of resentment may arise. Parents may even feel anger and withdrawal, and marital strain may occur. Parents in this stage will often fluctuate between periods of hope and disappointment over the course of adapting to the diagnosis. The post-diagnosis stage is characterized by parents' searching for information about the disorder, and accessing support and treatment. It is important for parents to learn as much as possible about the disorder and its treatment through methods of self-education. It is at this time that they may learn that there is a lack of community services for their child, and joining an advocacy group may be necessary to help them to cope. During the first years following diagnosis, parents are particularly vulnerable to quick fixes or miracle cures. Parents' desire to find a solution should be acknowledged; however, professionals should take care not to encourage them to actively pursue unsubstantiated "cures" for the disorder.

In the final stage of acceptance and adaptation, both positive and negative consequences may occur. One advantage to the diagnosis is that it provides an explanation for the behavior of the child, and aids parents in acceptance that they were not to blame for the disorder. Another advantage of the diagnostic process is that it provides access to other parents, sources of support, sources of treatment, and understanding by others in similar life situations. The disadvantage of the diagnosis is that its very nature implies that the child will never be "normal," thus creating worry and pessimism for the future. Other disadvantages of the diagnostic process include the public's lack of understanding of the condition, leading to negative interactions between the child and other people. Parents may become frustrated and confused by the social stigma caused by a lack of public awareness of the disorder, and as a result isolate themselves from significant others.

Research indicates that the early years for parents of children with autism are characterized by emotional distress related to the discovery that the child is disabled. Working through the initial period of grief while addressing the challenge of aiding the child in the home, finding community services, and anticipating the child's future is critical to parents' acceptance of the diagnosis and their ability to develop feelings of empowerment.

Early diagnosis and assessment is widely considered to be the first step in helping parents develop awareness of the challenges they must face. Although the cause of the disorder is unknown, parents should understand that the problem did not result from improper parenting or related environmental circumstances. This will enable the parents to move beyond feelings of self-blame and guilt for their child's difficulties.

Cary's tips

- Seek out professional advice for yourself and your child. Remember, you are the consumer, and you have the right to ask questions and form your own opinion with regard to treatment.

- Don't fall for "miracle cures" that have not been proven to be effective. They are costly and often do not work. Be sure to do your own research to determine the best course of action for your child.

SOMETHING TO TALK ABOUT

1. How has having a child with autism affected your relationship with your significant other?

2. What has been the hardest part for your marriage/relationship?

3. What is one thing you could start doing today that would have a major positive impact on your relationship with your spouse?

4. Is there anything that you need from your spouse that he or she might not realize that would make a big difference to your overall happiness?

5. What are the things that you and your spouse argue about the most or that are most stressful for your relationship? Why?

6. Describe the reaction of family members when you informed them of your child's diagnosis? How did their reaction affect you?

7. What are some ways to deal with family members who deny the diagnosis?

8. What are some ways to educate family members about autism and related disorders?

9. Which of your family members has been most supportive/ least supportive?

10. How can you help your family members understand how to interact with an autistic child, and understand his or her needs, without seeming bossy or offensive? (Remember, these are people that aren't going to just disappear!)

11. What are some suggestions for attending family gatherings with your child with autism?

12. Why might it be important to include family members in major decisions involving your child with autism?

REFLECTION ACTIVITY

- Schedule a time for a relationship inventory (see Appendix B) with your spouse or significant other. Set goals to spend time together and review monthly.

- Hold a family council. Create an agenda ahead of time and discuss everyone's concerns.

5.

Oh, Brother: Siblings and the Spectrum

Angelique, Matthew (6), and Caleb (4)

Matthew is a busy man. Whenever I'm not at home with him he has fit after fit. He is highly aggressive and very bossy. At 18 months he wasn't really talking yet. It seemed he had one word that he'd use for an entire week and then totally forget about it. Caleb, his brother, was born around that time. A couple of months later I noticed Matthew flapping his hands and walking on his toes when he got excited; he looked like a bird. I thought perhaps he couldn't hear because he never responded to anybody. He had major tantrums. When I wasn't at home with him he would headbutt the floor and freak out.

Early Intervention was already coming out to the house to see my younger son, Caleb, for other reasons, so I mentioned my concerns about Matthew to them as well. After evaluating him, the doctor told me Matthew had Pervasive Developmental Disorder-Not Otherwise Specified (PDD-NOS). I didn't really understand what the implications were and didn't investigate any further. No one told me the kind of services or help that was available. A couple of years ago I started to look into it more and realized PDD was in essence autism—just under a different name. Matthew was diagnosed at age two and we didn't do anything for him until he was four.

With Caleb, they are also saying that he might have autism. We're trying to get the ball rolling earlier this time and see if we can't get him diagnosed. As far as symptoms, Caleb never had tantrums like Matthew, but he toe-walks excessively. He talks in a monotone and he wanders aimlessly like he has no clue where he's going. He doesn't pay attention to anything. He's higher functioning than Matthew but he definitely shows traits of autism, just not the same ones we saw with Matthew. His speech is delayed as well. There's certainly a difference between those two.

As you can imagine, life is hectic. I make appointment after appointment for both Matthew and Caleb, and go with the flow. I try to maintain a positive attitude and not get discouraged. My third child, Dylan, is a typically functioning two-year-old. At this time, my main goal is to do whatever is best for all my sons. I want to make sure they get what they need and have every opportunity available.

Angelique's tips

- Talk to other parents; make friends with people that also have children with autism.

- Offer your support to other parents. Ask them how they are doing, how their child is doing, and check in with them regularly.

- Find at least one caring friend who is willing to listen, no matter what kind of day you've both had.

ԳՉ

Chuck, Kay (11), and Kyle (9)

Kyle is so set in his ways it's beginning to take a toll on his sister Kay. He is so rigid and inflexible that we end up catering to his needs rather than addressing hers. Life is a lot simpler if we don't fight him. A lot of the time we aren't able to do the things she likes to do because Kyle doesn't want to do them. Novel situations are hard; we have tried to go to the city pool and Busch Gardens (an amusement park) but we left after an hour because Kyle was getting antsy. Things like that are difficult on Kay because she wants to stay, but Kyle becomes overwhelmed so we have to leave.

We don't have any type of respite or babysitting service so one of us is always with Kyle. We play tag; I come in the door as my wife goes out. Whenever she's at work I'm home, and vice versa. My daughter has never seen both of us together at any major event of hers—she likes acting and activities like that, and although one of us is always there for her we never show up together because someone has to stay with Kyle.

Kyle is very affectionate and now that his sister is older she is accustomed to our situation and understands that there are issues. She's still fairly young though, and it's rough for her. Frankly, it's hard to deal with even if you're an adult. She's very patient and tries to help Kyle out as much as she can. At school she is president of the Leo Club (an offshoot of the Lions Club) and part of the group's purpose is to do charitable work within the community. She has decided to make everything Kyle does into club service projects. For instance, the Leo Club made Valentine's Day cards for all the kids at Kyle's school. Kyle is also involved with therapeutic horseback riding, so Kay is planning on doing something related to that for their next venture. To me, her involvement shows maturity and commitment to helping her brother.

ॐ

Connie, Chris (15), and Charlotte (8)

Chris is introverted and mellow; he's also 15, though, which could explain that attitude. He likes to be in his room and he enjoys a lot of typical teenage stuff like action adventure movies and video games. There aren't a lot of older kids around the neighborhood he can hang out with, so he's pretty much on his own when he's at home. On the other hand, Charlotte is headstrong and active; always getting into things she's not supposed to. She enjoys watching TV and movies, but is more interested in doing arts and crafts such as drawing and cutting. She gets along with her brother and older sister most of the time.

Back when he was first tested, we were told Chris was developmentally delayed. At three and a half years old we met with a developmental pediatrician who gave him the PDD label. She told us that the school would take care of things and to let them handle it, and sent us on our way. She did a thorough job as far as testing him, but the follow-up information for us was terrible. I left her office believing that after a couple years of remedial work in school everything would be fine—that was the impression she gave us. No big deal, right?

Behaviorally, Chris has always been quiet and reserved, so we weren't dealing with a lot of out-of-control behaviors. I saw more of it than they did at school because at school they were constantly moving from activity to activity. He'd come home and be tired, and winding down from the day, so I'd see a little more acting out. Overall, considering what my daughter has put me through he has been well behaved.

Charlotte is the complete opposite of Chris as far as personalities go. Whereas I could sit Chris down in front of the TV and he'd watch the *Star Wars* trilogy back to back without any problem, Charlotte requires constant attention. I could always find something to occupy Chris but with Charlotte that's not an option. Once she makes up her mind about something she has to have it her way or else. She is like a little pit bull—if she gets her teeth into something she doesn't let go. Charlotte is aggressive and much more determined to have her own way than Chris ever was. Her behavior used to be much worse than it is currently, though. I joke with everybody that having Chris *never* prepared me for Charlotte.

By the time Charlotte hit 18 months I was calling the school requesting for her to be tested. Although the children were quite different in personality, I was having flashbacks of the mannerisms Chris had when he was younger. No one could convince me that she didn't have a problem, even though they did seem a bit hesitant to slap an autism label on her. Similar to Chris, she started out as "developmentally delayed" and then received the PDD/autism label later. Charlotte is also classified as having Oppositional Defiancy Disorder.

In school the teachers didn't know how to handle Charlotte's aggression any better than we did. They did introduce her to Picture Exchange Communication System (PECS), though, which she loves to this day. If she happens to find her old PECS pictures lying around she'll break them out all over the place. You can't take them away. She could verbally communicate to a certain point but because of her behavior PECS seemed to be a good match, especially when she became frustrated trying to tell us something. Her language started coming in as time went on, and we used PECS as a back-up when things started getting a bit unruly. We also incorporated some Floor Time activities. Charlotte made excellent progress with play skills during that time. She learned how to use toys appropriately and take turns.

When Charlotte began school she became extremely defiant. When she was six years old, I became active in the local support group and started meeting more parents. A friend of mine from the group who ran an Applied Behavioral Analysis (ABA) home program mentioned that one of her therapists also worked at a place called Behave'n Day (see www.behavenkids.com), and suggested it might be a good fit for Charlotte. She encouraged me to go and check it out even though they didn't deal specifically with autism. By that time, I was practically begging someone to tell me what to do, since neither the school nor the doctors had the first clue about what to do, and nothing I was trying on my own seemed to be working very well either. I decided I had nothing to lose; I was desperate and knew we needed to do something as soon as possible. I went out to take a look at the program half-heartedly but came home after seeing what they could accomplish with a resolve to do whatever was necessary to get her in.

To attend the program the autism label wasn't sufficient so that was when the psychiatrists labeled Charlotte with Oppositional Defiancy Disorder. At first I thought, "Another label, doesn't she have enough already?"

Then that night she had this massive meltdown and I decided at that moment I didn't care what label they put on her, she was going to that program. I threw my reservations about labels out the window. Thankfully she was accepted with the additional diagnosis and Medicaid covered the cost.

After Charlotte had been attending Behave'n Day for about six months the stress level in our house went down dramatically. They worked with Charlotte and the other kids to set up a strict discipline plan with specific consequences for inappropriate actions. It was up to the parents to be *consistent* with the rules. After completing the program a lot of my friends who hadn't seen Charlotte in a few months were shocked when they saw her. Their reactions were priceless. They would say things like, "Oh my gosh, she's not bouncing off the walls, she's not freaking out, and she's not having temper tantrums. What happened?" Overall, even though the behaviors weren't completely eliminated it was the best thing we ever did for her.

Once we implemented the program and consistently enforced expectations things got better and better. We were able to incorporate the program's standards at home and when we were out in public. For Charlotte it was a great fit, but for Chris it wouldn't have been appropriate. Other than that I haven't followed any specific treatment path with Chris or Charlotte, I've just tried to give them both the best educational foundation I could, and hoped for the best.

Connie's tips

- Educate yourself. Attend workshops and conferences, read books, and go on websites.
- Compare information with other parents, and network.
- Know your rights under the law.

ॐ

Jaimee, Matthew (4), and Jake (2)

When Matthew, my oldest son, was 14 months old, we started seeing some strange behavior. He would line up his toys or place them in a circle. If you happened to knock one over, he would scream. Around this age Matthew learned his ABCs and 123s, which he would repeat constantly. Once we taught him to count, he counted everything. Often he would begin counting something, then we would go to dinner or leave for an hour or so, and when we came back, Matthew would know the exact number he had left off at and continue counting again. If he played with his toys he would sort them according to color, count them or put them together so they formed the shape of each letter in the alphabet rather than using them as they were intended.

To be honest I really don't know when his speech stopped developing. He started saying single words at the usual time but he never went any further. He started learning how to read and write, and could recite whole passages from movies, but in everyday life would only grunt, or say yes or no. Sometimes if I asked him a question he didn't know how to answer, he would just use dialogue from one of his videos.

When I found I was pregnant again I was thrilled—for the first day. After that, I had an indescribable fear that was with me day and night. I began thinking having another baby might have a detrimental effect on Matthew because Matthew needed my undivided attention. I became so stressed I started getting seizures and migraines. No one else seemed to understand Matthew's neediness. By being pregnant, I felt like I wasn't going to be able to be there for him when he needed me most. I suppose that was my subconscious telling me I had more to deal with than I knew.

Late in the pregnancy I became very ill and I spent two weeks in hospital while they tried to stabilize me. I was not allowed to move and saw Matthew only twice during the whole ordeal. It broke my heart knowing I was not there. I fretted, wondering if he'd be okay. The need to protect him was overwhelming. After Jake was born it was another week before I was able to leave hospital and I was still not doing so well. My stress level was very high and I felt like I was going to fall apart.

In the weeks following Jake's birth, Matthew's behavior changed very little except for becoming a little more obsessive. He now displayed a pronounced dislike for socializing with other children. During a visit to the local health nurse for Jake, I mentioned Matthew's unusual behaviors and the nurse referred me to the Developmental Assessment Service. I agreed to an evaluation, but was placed on a long waiting list.

After several additional phone calls to the Department of Human Services, Matthew's assessment appointment was scheduled for over a year later. Our lives were on hold while we waited for a diagnosis or explanation for our son's behaviors. My husband Gary insisted that Matthew's problems were nothing more than being a little slower than most his age and soon the problems would level out.

When we were given the results from the evaluation there were certain aspects in which Matthew rated particularly poorly. In other areas of the examination, his abilities were off the charts. The writing was on the wall from that point on for me. I anticipated the outcome would be autism, although the findings were inconclusive. Gary was nowhere near ready to accept such a finding. No other services were rendered at that time for our son.

Following the assessment Gary and I fought constantly over anything and everything. His anger still has not subsided. Although he privately concedes that Matthew is autistic, he refuses to tell anyone about Matthew's disorder until the official diagnosis. I once inquired about the possibility of paying to get the diagnosis privately so we can finally move on, but there is even a six-month waiting list for that, so it wouldn't really make much of a difference.

Since that time Matthew has started kindergarten. Things went smoothly first but it wasn't long before his anxieties began to kick in. At the school, the tables are rearranged on a daily basis, so each day he went in to the room looking for something familiar only to find everything different—the set-up was unpredictable. Then the social aspects of attending school began to bother him. Finally, he became so overloaded with stress and anxiety that he would have meltdowns in the car every morning.

The first time Matthew had a meltdown on the way to school was the worst. I drove Matthew and Jake, who was now 16 months old, to kindergarten. When I opened the car door to let Matthew out, he refused and started crying. After five minutes of coaxing and pleading, I undid his seatbelt and had to practically drag him out of the car while he screamed and kicked. All the other parents simply walked past. Some even stared at us with a bit of a smirk on their faces, adding to my feeling of helplessness.

Next Matthew dropped to the ground and wouldn't move. I didn't know what to do. I couldn't carry both boys because Matthew was being so resistant. Ten more minutes passed as I tried to negotiate with Matthew to go inside while he thrashed and screamed to get back in the car. By now, most of the parents had dropped their children off, walked past me, and left. I was nearly in tears and wanted to fall apart myself. Two parents in the car next to me finally offered to watch Jake while I carried Matthew into the building. I thanked them profusely and jogged inside with Matthew over my shoulder.

When we got in the classroom the screaming became even more intense. The teacher came over with a smile and tried to peel Matthew off me. Meanwhile one of the parents was tapping on the window signaling to me that Jake was crying. Two minutes later I was walking out of the school, biting my bottom lip as I was met by one of the parents who let me know Jake was really upset. By the time I got to the car, Jake was hysterical and I could not settle him. I thought I'd just hurry up and get him home, which was only a few blocks away, rather than comfort him there. I thanked the parents again and jumped in the car. As I drove I had the feeling I was on the verge of a meltdown myself.

Before I had driven a couple of meters, Jake had started vomiting and choking, so I pulled over, turned him upside down and emptied his mouth. Getting back in the car after settling Jake down, the realization hit me that this was my life and at the moment my life was a disaster. I wondered how I could take care of these children who I loved so much, but who had so many needs.

During a home visit from the child psychologist a couple of months ago, he started asking questions about Jake. "Did he play? Was he always so focused? How was his speech going?" The truth was devastating for me to admit. "No. He has never played. Yes. He can sit there for an hour without looking away. Jake is 19 months and hasn't ever spoken a single word."

Following that visit Jake was diagnosed with moderate autism. Thinking about it literally makes me ill. I fear I may never know what it is like to raise a "normal" child. Although my marriage is falling apart I have at times even considered taking my chances by having another child; despite that I could get very sick again and die during pregnancy or lose the baby, my soul craves the idea of normalcy. Whether it is right or wrong, this overwhelming desire to raise a normal child never leaves.

In the meantime, I have two very beautiful boys. They are both very funny and happy children. I love them very much and know they love me. My marriage is on a knife edge, but our child psychologist has been slipping in a little marriage counseling when he can and that has helped. I really didn't think I could ever manage a child with special needs, but I have surprised myself. When things get rough I console myself with the fact that I know I am doing everything I can for my children. No matter what life throws my way, I will always be there for my children, as long as they need me.

Jaimee's tips

- In the early stages post-diagnosis, don't get overwhelmed by all the information you will be bombarded with.

- Deal with the specialists and professionals as you would if this were your occupation.

- Keep organized, maintain an accurate diary, and file all reports, notes and letters so you can find contact details and references when you need to.

CR

Jennifer, Colin (4), and Cameron (4)

Our house is in a constant state of chaos. With the twins there are a lot of tantrums and meltdowns over their perceived order of how they want their day to be. Currently, they have an obsession with Spider Man clothing. If I don't find the right shirt or I can't figure out exactly what they want then they get frustrated and have meltdowns. Because I also have an older son with Tourette's and Obsessive-Compulsive Disorder (OCD), sensory issues and a low tolerance of noise are added to the array of challenges we face on a daily basis. I run around trying to put out fires and figure out who needs what, what obsessions I can help, and what aches I can soothe, while trying to maintain my own sense of sanity.

On the day the twins were born, I realized something wasn't right. When I checked on them in the nursery I told the attendants something was wrong with the babies. The nurses said, "They're fine. They're perfectly healthy. You've just had twins and you need to relax." I took them back to my room and, as I was looking at them, I had this uncomfortable feeling something was wrong. Maybe it was because when my first son was born he looked me right in the eye and bonded with me. The twins just lay there, unresponsive.

As they grew, many milestones were not met. They failed numerous hearing tests, had constant ear infections, sinus infections, projectile vomiting, and frequent diarrhea. According to an immunologist we consulted years later, they had a reaction to cow's milk protein which in turn affected their digestive systems. The poor kids were so sick, and to top it off I would send them to daycare because I was working full-time and they caught every kind of sickness imaginable. They received antibiotics continuously throughout their first year of life.

Actually, the daycare provider was a blessing in disguise. Even though I knew something was wrong with the twins, you are always told twins are slow to develop so don't worry. However, she advised me to call Birth to 3 and they completed a full evaluation. At 17 months my boys did not meet six of their developmental milestones and were performing at the level of six-month-olds. Nobody put a label on them at that point, though.

For the next year, each boy received one hour of services each per week. I thought, "I need something more than this." So I asked the doctors, "What do you think is wrong?" but they couldn't tell me anything except that Colin and Cameron were developmentally delayed. I thought maybe they had ADHD since they were very active, and contacted a neurologist in West Hartford. My husband took time off work so we could attend the appointment together, but I seriously considered calling it off. I doubted they could do anything for the boys because they were so young. The neurologist observed them for about 20 minutes and then he said, "I'm going to tell this to you point blank. I'm not one to be kind with words but I have to tell you your twins have autism." Cameron had mild autism and Colin's diagnosis was moderate. At that minute it was as if the floor ate me up.

That was definitely one of the worst days of our lives. We were totally in shock and didn't know where to turn. We weren't given anything to help us through that. You almost need a grief counselor. We did what most parents do: chose not to believe it at first and got a second opinion. It came as a relief when the second doctor was of the opinion that they were merely developmentally delayed.

Years later, we questioned the doctor about the second diagnosis. We needed to get the label of autism to qualify for the services in town. She told us that she gave us that diagnosis to placate us and to make us happy. "I didn't want to put a label on them, but they do have autism," she told us. That is where a lot of parents go wrong in Connecticut. The medical profession does a severe disservice to these children if it does not confer the label of autism. PDD is another word for autism, but if you don't have the specific word "autism" in the diagnosis, the child will not receive funding for 32 hours a week of therapy or a paraprofessional in the classroom, or extra speech therapy or occupational therapy. The parents who have the most difficulty are those who don't have a definitive diagnosis.

Today both boys have spontaneous language, but it's still difficult to have a conversation with them. For example, if I asked one of them a question like, "Where is your brother?" he would have a hard time responding. They also have a tendency to perseverate (say the same thing over and over) so I'll say, "One time" to which they repeat "One time." If I am going somewhere with them I have to tell them five to ten minutes ahead of time where we are going so they can prepare. They cannot transition from one place to another without having a meltdown if I don't give them a proper warning, and with each boy weighing 45 pounds it really taxes me because they both melt down at the same time.

For the most part, I don't go many places with Colin and Cameron. We don't visit other people's homes because my children are likely to destroy them. If I'm out in public people we don't know look at me as if to say, "Why can't you control your children?" Nothing the parenting books suggest works with autistic children—I could scream or put them in time out or say, "*No!*" over and over, but it would have no effect, so for discipline we redirect.

When we do venture out of the house, in addition to dirty looks I get looks of pity, which is another reason why we seldom go out. My boys don't attend playgroups because they don't play with toys, they play with furniture. I have no lamps in my living room because they have broken at least eight of them. I keep thinking next time they will learn to respect the lamps, but it never happens. My home is bare; I don't have any knick-knacks lying around. We have chain locks on all the doors, childproof doorknobs, and have installed gates outside assuming that if one of the boys did get outside the gate would at least slow them down, if not stop them. My husband lost one of the twins once; he hid, so escape is a very real fear. They've run into the road before and I've repeatedly tried to teach them about consequences but they don't understand.

One of the boys didn't speak until age two and I remember someone told me to try Di-methyl-glycine (DMG)—a food supplement. The night we tried it, Colin started saying his first word: newspaper. He said, "Look at the newspaper" over and over again. I was so happy he was saying anything I didn't care if he was saying it correctly. The DMG didn't do much for Cameron. I'm definitely pro-supplement and willing to try herbal remedies. My children have had a lot of infections so we see an immunologist in New Jersey who determined what they have overgrowths of and the right dosage of whatever we use. I think a lot of people try and figure out what works on their own, which can be dangerous. My doctor said that people who have done chelation on their own have come into her practice with blood in their urine because of kidney failure. Be careful with any medication, herbal or not, and make sure you have a professional on your side. Some kids definitely need medication, but it has to be administered correctly; if it isn't you could damage your child permanently on top of the autism.

We feel fortunate the boys were diagnosed so young. They are both enrolled in our town's preschool program for special needs children. Each class has three teachers and ten children with approximately a third of the kids being typically developing. I watched a video of one of my sons with his peers and it's incredible to see because the autistic children closely watch what their peers do. The children with autism look at them for clues for songs and story time, and also for confirmation, as if to say, "Should I do that?" For that reason I think it's crucial for any educational program to include normal-functioning peers.

The program the twins are in is amazing—the school took these exceptionally gifted children who wanted to help special needs children and put them in the classroom together. The students are hand-picked to model appropriate behavior in social situations. The school is incredible; the teachers are loving but firm. I was even able to coordinate my potty training efforts with them and now my children are fully potty trained. That was one of my biggest fears—that they'd never be potty trained—but because of the school's willingness to coordinate the effort it worked. Even with the additional effort required because the boys are in separate classrooms the school was there for me.

The hardest part for me was accepting that Cameron and Colin are not ever going to be "normal." When I started admitting that to myself was when I started reaching out to other parents of autistic children and connecting with them. As I heard their stories and shared mine I started getting stronger and it made me say, "Wow, I'm not so different." Remarkably, just down the street there are three other people going through the same things as me and I made friends with them.

We live in a relatively large town, so in our school district there are quite a few children with autism. Once I started talking to their parents and bonding with them I didn't feel so isolated. I've kept my old friends to an extent, but I feel such a connection with my new friends. It is so important to have the support of other parents if you have a newly diagnosed child. Other parents in your area that have gone through it can be an invaluable resource and can help you navigate the intricacies of the system. You can have all the counselors and psychiatrists in the world, but when you can literally talk to someone who has already walked in your shoes you feel united with them immediately. They know what you've gone through and they understand your pain; you don't even have to talk about it.

I just got off the phone with somebody who saw the bumper sticker for "Unlocking Autism" on my car. The man came up to my husband and said his daughter-in-law and son had a child with autism and he wanted someone to call them. I gave her a call and she was crying she was so relieved to have someone who finally understood what she was experiencing to talk to—we connected instantly. She didn't know any other parents with autistic children. You need that. If you have at least one person to talk to you won't feel so lost and alone.

Currently, Cameron and Colin are doing wonderfully. I think I've done the right things. They make gains daily and are constantly growing; they haven't become stagnant. Most parents of autistic children I speak to say their kids make progress every day; it's just in smaller increments than a typically developing child would make. Don't take anything for granted. Look at every little special thing they do, recognize the positive gains, and appreciate everything. They are absorbing everything like a sponge and people do autistic children an injustice by thinking they're not understanding or getting it. They get it, they just can't speak it. Remember that there are severely autistic children that have no speech, but they understand. They are often underestimated.

Jennifer's tips

- If you are the parent the two things that you need are a computer and Internet access. I don't care if you have to beg, borrow, or steal to get one; computers are an essential and invaluable resource to get the support you need, especially if you live in a rural area.

- Celebrate the small changes.

ơ

Jennifer, Ryan (4), and Kyle (4)

With twins the chance of both having autism is much higher than for regular siblings. Ryan is very sweet and loving. He is bright in a different way, wanting to know how everything works and the mechanics of things. He is starting to write his own name—before Kyle—and has recently started counting. He has made a lot of headway. We started seeing some language come in about six months ago, whereas he never had any before.

When we took the boys for their two-year-old well-check neither was speaking at all. Unfortunately, our pediatrician didn't have the best bedside manner so rather than explaining that she was worried about my children, and encouraging me to have them evaluated, she just said right off, "You need to see a child psychologist; take them there right now." She didn't give us any indication that she thought they were showing signs of autism, nothing specific, so we weren't too concerned.

Since they were both boys, they were born early and they were twins, I figured their language would come eventually. I was offended by that doctor's suggestion to take my boys to a psychologist. Nevertheless, by the time they were two and a half I started getting really concerned. Ryan still wasn't speaking, so we decided to get them evaluated.

In the school district in Las Vegas where we lived at the time, they had a program for parents who were worried their kids weren't developing properly, so we took them there for the tests. It was a horrible day. Everybody was so nice, but Ryan had a tantrum (screaming, non-stop crying, aggression—it sounded like he was being beaten when no one was touching him) the whole time we were there. He just couldn't handle the situation. His protest made testing him adequately impossible. I'm glad they were able to see what we went through every day with him though. That morning, before we left the house, I thought, "He's going to go in there and be this perfect angel, and they will say, 'Okay lady what are you making up?'" So it was reassuring to see some of his typical behaviors come out.

About four months passed between when we suspected something was wrong and the actual diagnosis. The school district recommended we put the boys in the special education preschool in the local district. That was pretty much all they did for us. They gave us the diagnosis and sent us on our way. We didn't know where to go or what to do; they gave us no information about other resources. We were on our own. The boys were in that school for about a month until we moved to Idaho and our world changed. From what I've found, I think the services here in Idaho are wonderful. There's a lot out there for these kids. We were apprehensive about moving at first, having just received the diagnoses. We figured it was going to be so hard for them, but it's been the best thing for all of us in the long run.

My husband is an extremely wonderful father but he didn't believe anything was wrong. He figured they're going to talk eventually and he went through a denial phase. I never did. I didn't want to say it, but I knew there was something going on. I had never heard about autism, I didn't know the signs. When they told me the diagnosis it was devastating. I went through probably three or four months where I didn't go outside; it took over my life in a bad way. Now it has taken over in a good way. You can't prepare for something like this to happen, but you deal with it and do the best you can.

Ryan vs Kyle

For Ryan, the hardest part is socialization and trying to communicate. We couldn't take him anywhere until about six months ago. Therapy has been so helpful. When he was first diagnosed we couldn't go anywhere because he would just tantrum most of the time. His tantrums, transitions, and anxiety are much better now; he's come such a long way.

Kyle has an amazing amount of language now, he's really talking. He's just a character, always trying to make us laugh. Kyle is delayed in his emotional development, but his cognitive skills are improving. Sometimes I think he needs Intensive Behavior Intervention (IBI) more than Ryan. He has come a long way too. Ryan is more quiet and shy and pensive, and much more aware of his setting and what's going on around him. He's always looking around checking out what's going on, seeing who's walking in and walking out. Kyle is more happy-go-lucky and not quite as serious.

The interaction between Ryan and Kyle has gotten a lot better since we began therapy. Like most siblings, they fight all the time; I guess it's a brother thing. Kyle is the more affectionate one, he wants to hug and kiss Ryan but Ryan wants to be left alone. For a while they weren't interacting at all. I often wonder what it would be like if Ryan didn't have Kyle. I think Kyle's example is really important to Ryan's development because he's starting to copy Kyle and do the things that Kyle does. Having a model is so important. I think Ryan would probably still be in his own little world if it weren't for Kyle.

CR

Kim, Cody (9), and Dillon (7)

Cody and Dillon are as opposite as night and day. Cody is generally very happy and is content to play computer games or read books. He keeps to himself but loves it if you sit and watch him. Dillon is compulsive about everything. One has Asperger's and the other was diagnosed with high-functioning autism. They are two very separate children with different needs.

Both boys were mainstreamed right into school, so I didn't tell people about their diagnoses. Most people probably wouldn't guess either of them had autism since they are both so high functioning; Dillon is a "stimmer" though—lots of hand flapping. Dillon has always been different. When he was born I called my mom and said, "I don't know what it is but he doesn't like me. Mark my words; I'm going to find something." The biggest issues with Cody are he doesn't engage in appropriate contact and has difficulty with social interactions. Cody knew all the state capitals by the time he was two and a half years old but he couldn't ask for a cookie. He never pointed to things or asked, "What's that?"

My husband and I took Cody to a pediatric specialist, who said that there was nothing wrong with him. Since he was able to say the names of states and their capitals, and could sit and play with balls, as far as the doctor was concerned he was fine. We left the office thinking maybe we were overreacting. However, right before his third birthday we took him to a preschool screening, and that's where they made the diagnosis. I knew as I sat there in the waiting room that something was wrong. All the other kids were sitting there next to their moms and were well behaved, but Cody was bouncing off the walls. He knew his alphabet and all the academic stuff they asked him about but there was no way he would sit and do an eye test. The director took me to a separate room, held my hand and said, "We think he has…" and I finished her sentence and said "autism," which was odd because I knew nothing about autism. I don't even know where it came from but I knew. His actual diagnosis is PDD.

Both boys have made great progress since they were diagnosed. Socially, Dillon is so far ahead of everyone it's awkward. His favorite thing to talk about is CDs. He knows every track number of every CD he owns (he has over 100). I think other kids look at him and say "eew." He has a much better time with older people. He'd rather be with adults, talking about music, than with kids his own age. Cody wants friends, but the kids sense that he's slightly different. We recently moved to a smaller town, and the closer environment has helped, especially for Dillon. The city doesn't have the resources a larger school system would have, but they've been very good about working with me and overall I've been satisfied.

Earlier this year I emailed Temple Grandin (see Recommended Reading section) and she actually called me back. As I described my concerns about the boys to her, I mentioned that Cody is into computers and would spend all day long at the computer if I let him. She advised me to limit his use and recommended I choose games like *Sim City* because he wants to be a builder. She cautioned, "Unless you limit that they *become* that." In regard to Dillon's obsession with CDs she encouraged me to get him more involved with music. I was so grateful for the insight of someone who has actually lived through what my boys are experiencing. Temple is an example and inspiration to parents everywhere and speaking with her was truly the event of my summer.

Kim's tips

- Hang in there! Tomorrow is another day and it really does get better. There is hope for these children.

- Take the pressure off yourself, remember you are not raising normal kids—this is tough! You are doing okay. You are not a bad parent.

CR

Kim, Justin (8), and Caitlynn (6)

Justin is energetic to say the least. He wakes up between 6:30 and 7:00 a.m., at which time I dose him with 54 mg of Concerta and 10 mg of Ritalin. Within half an hour the drugs should begin to take effect; if not I know it's going to be a long morning. I wrestle him into clothes, force some nourishment into him, and shove him out the door for school. Actually, I walk him the 1.51 km to his school because we live so close he does not qualify for bussing, and accompany him to his classroom. Usually I have a brief conversation with his educational assistant and then go home. After school I do the walk again, only by this time the effects of his medications are wearing off. At 6:00 p.m. he gets Risperdal and Melatonin to help him go to sleep. On a good night he is down by 9:30; on a bad night he might be up until 3 a.m.

Caitlynn is mellower than Justin but she is much more scatterbrained. Justin usually wakes her up with his screaming in the morning; therefore she is also an early bird. By 7:00 a.m. she comes down and has breakfast. Oftentimes she cannot find her clothes or her shoes. At school she sometimes forgets that she cannot sing in the middle of class. She refuses to eat lunch. When she gets home she does her homework, which she loves, and then goes to play with her Dora dolls. Her autism is considered at the high-functioning level and very mild.

With Justin I always knew there was something that just was not right with him. He was two months old and when all the other infants in his playgroups were cooing, he was not. At four months he was still very floppy and never babbled. I kept talking to my pediatrician and I was told many times that I read too many books and was looking for problems. After the first year it became increasingly apparent Justin was not developing like other kids.

At his one-year check-up the doctors were concerned over his lack of weight gain. Again, I was advised not to worry if he had some speech delays because if they persisted a referral to a specialist would be made at his 18-month appointment. Following the 18-month appointment he was indeed referred to a developmental pediatrician as well as a speech therapist. The developmental pediatrician referred us to a genetics counselor and we still see her once a year. When Justin was six years old, the diagnosis of autism was made.

With Caitie the process of obtaining a diagnosis was very different. An infant development program we attended recommended that I have her assessed because some of her reactions were indicative of autism. A team of experts, including a psychiatrist, a psychologist, a social worker, an occupational therapist, and a speech therapist, watched Caitie for about a half an hour and agreed that she too had autism. I am now seeking a more comprehensive assessment to make sure this quick conclusion is correct.

My reaction to both diagnoses was tears. I cried several hours each time the diagnosis was given. After that I threw myself into obtaining services for Justin and Caitie, and working with them on speech, nutrition, and occupational therapy exercises. I also talked a lot to the resource people at the daycare that they attended. They offered the most support of all.

How has my life changed? An easier question might be, "How has my life not changed?" I think I have become a more understanding parent out of all of this. I never question why a child in a mall is freaking out any more; instead I think, "Thank goodness it is not me today." I rejoice in every triumph, no matter how small. I grieve for the "typical" child that I do not have, but also rejoice for the children I do have. My perspective has changed and it has made me into a better person.

As far as my family in general goes, they have changed quite a bit. I have two other children who do not know the joy of having a brother who does not get as angry and who does not have to take boatloads of medication. My youngest daughter does not know the joy of having a big sister who does fun stuff with her. Through all of this, I also think that my other children have learned to have patience, to do things creatively with their siblings, and to have compassion for those who are different.

I believe that God sent me these two children for a purpose. It is all in his plan and it will become even clearer as they grow. I have not figured it all out yet, but I know that I have become stronger due to these trials. So perhaps that is the purpose and this is not a random thing, and I was picked to care for these special children because I have the courage to do so.

Kim's tips

- Take all the help that is offered, such as respite, occupational therapy, speech therapy, and child care.
- Get things started as quickly as possible as far as treatments are concerned.

- Take time for yourself and make sure that you don't lose yourself in the process of helping your child.

- Join support groups, publicly and online.

- Talk about your child to others—it helps!

- Get a second opinion if you are not convinced. Be persistent about services and always stay on top of them.

CR

Leslie, Jared (9), and Alyssa (7)

Jared is our firstborn child and he has a younger sister, Alyssa. Alyssa is typical, but I should eat my words to say she is easier. There are two totally different sets of needs there. Jared is a very loving, sweet child, and I think everyone that knows him would agree. On that note, I can't say he doesn't have difficult moments. Jared is very stubborn and has limited speech, but he can communicate using words, pictures, and some sign language.

I don't have a lot of time for anyone else except my immediate family any more. My friends sort of faded into the background, because they know I am busy and overwhelmed with what is going on in my life. I am also nervous in public about what other people will think; and I'm constantly worried about what Jared will do. I can't predict when his mood swings or erratic behaviors will occur as they come without warning. We recently went on our first family vacation in ten years. Something as simple as traveling to an unfamiliar location was terrifying because we just didn't know what to expect.

As Alyssa gets older she understands more and more about how to handle Jared. He used to take his frustrations out on Alyssa and would often hit her. She is just starting to comprehend what it means to have an autistic brother. She is also realizing that she will have to act like the older sibling because she knows her brother is not capable of that.

I've noticed the extent that what I say to Jared in front of Alyssa is crucial because she is beginning to pick up on how we handle things. For example, when Jared is aggressive, we sometimes have to straddle him and repeat "Time out," until he calms down and stops trying to hit. The other day he was hitting his sister so she turned to him, held his hand and said, "Now Jared that is hitting your sister," like her father or I would do. Jared actually responded to her, which amazed me. She is mirroring the things we do and learning how to deal with his behaviors just as we are. In the past when Jared would hurt her, she would yell and become angry, and the whole situation would escalate. Now Alyssa is becoming more responsible and is taking it upon herself to try and help him. I am proud of how maturely she is handling things.

I choose not to remember what my life used to be like, and I don't really want to remember. My life is not about me any more, but about my children. The only thing I can focus on is how I can make it better for Jared and also how to help my daughter cope with a special needs brother. Our family has had to adjust to a new life, as well as a new normal. Sometimes we forget how stressful things are until we are around "normal families." We are slowing adjusting. My husband and I are in marriage counseling but we will stay together, because we are dedicated to raising our children and we do love each other very much.

CR

Liz, Travis (17), and Eric (14)

Life with Eric has been pretty hard on Travis, but Travis has been amazing with him to be perfectly honest. Recently Travis has been talking about asking a girl out. He wanted to take her to the natural history museum and see an IMAX movie. Since he didn't have his driver's license yet, I told him, "Eric and I will drive you. Then you and your date can go through the museum together and we can all watch the movie but we'll sit away from you." Travis said, "No Mom, I want any girl that I date to know about Eric and get to know Eric."

Once in a while I know Travis is embarrassed by the things Eric does, but I think he realizes that's how our family is. Travis has always been a great help and takes a lot of responsibility for his brother. He also helps with all the Autism Society activities. When we have our monthly meetings he helps with child care so other parents can attend. We make an effort to spend special time with Travis, too. My husband doesn't like to travel and Eric doesn't do well traveling either, so Travis and I go on vacation and take trips together. Sometimes Travis and his dad will do things together or occasionally just the three of us will do something. One-on-one time is so important. Travis is a great brother to Eric and does a lot to help the autism community as a whole and Eric in particular.

CR

Loren, Kyle (10), Ross (8), and Seth (5)

When I think back to the period after Ross was diagnosed, I wish I would have treated Kyle differently. We didn't brush him to the side on purpose, but we might have unintentionally because we were so caught up in helping Ross. We didn't really have that downtime or one-on-one time with Kyle. Kyle was only four and a half when Ross was diagnosed. We didn't have a clue what was going on ourselves, let alone try and explain it at a level a preschooler could understand.

I was pregnant with Seth, when I found out Ross had autism. He was a blessing for Ross because they played together wonderfully. When Seth was two and Ross was four they were the best of friends. They taught each other a great deal, including how to share and take turns. Ross didn't have the social skills, but he learned them along with Seth. If someone has a child with autism and thinks, "Oh no, I shouldn't have any more kids," I wouldn't necessarily agree. I'd say that it might even be helpful to have another child, although there is a certain risk associated with siblings of a child with autism. So far Seth is a typically developed five-year-old.

On the other hand, the whole situation is really hard on Kyle even now, and to make matters worse, he was just diagnosed this summer with ADHD, dyslexia, and anxiety. I don't know if his reaction towards Ross is associated with the responsibility of being the oldest or because of the way we treated him when he was younger. In hindsight, we could have spent more time with Kyle, but nobody gives you a manual and says, "Everything you need to know is in here, you will have no worries!"

We wonder about what the future will hold for Ross and if he will ever be able to live on his own. He's come a long way, but still can't manage some outwardly simple daily tasks. I have to remember he's only eight. We've got time.

Loren's tips

- Don't wait to begin Early Intervention—start as soon as possible.
- Research different treatments (diet, supplements, therapies).
- Join web rings.
- Know that you are not alone—there are many families who have "been there, done that."

CR

Maurine, Joshua (7), and Connor (5)

After Joshua was diagnosed one of the first things I did, was attend the National Vaccine Information (NVI) Conference in Washington, DC. I saw it advertised on the Internet. Joshua's brother Connor was born during the same month that Joshua was diagnosed. From the information we found on the Internet we decided to quit vaccinating Connor. So he had two vaccines when he was four months and that ended it, we never did any more. We honestly believe we saved at least one child. I went to this conference, and I came back and my head was just swimming with theories and therapies; we began doing ABA almost immediately thereafter.

South Carolina had great services available back then. We contacted "Baby Net" and found out Joshua was covered for 40 hours a week of therapy paid for by the state. Joshua had 40 hours of ABA for the entire first year. We really lucked out; Georgia didn't even have that. In South Carolina at that time, anyone who applied would have received the same amount of hours. A consultant worked with us to set up the program, too (all paid for). South Carolina doesn't pay so much any more, there are just too many kids.

Once Joshua entered the school system they reduced the amount of therapy. After that I had to fight for every hour. First the number dropped to 25 hours a week, but we were glad to have that. Then when he went into pre-K, that figure was cut to ten hours a week. When Joshua turned six they removed them completely. Services provided by outside consultants were eliminated and the schools began to handle the home programs themselves. There were just too many children in the system and the state couldn't afford the costs. We've been pretty lucky as far as that is concerned.

Financially our family has struggled horribly. Connor also received 40 hours of therapy a week because he had no spoken language at 18 months. We were hysterical trying to run two intensive programs at the same time. People were in and out of the house all day, which was really hard. We know a lot of people who have separate therapy rooms, but our little house is only 875 square feet so you can imagine with all that therapy going on at the same time it was very tight. We just didn't have the space, but we persevered.

Whereas Joshua had some language Connor had no words at all. Connor also couldn't clap, point, or wave; he couldn't do anything. At two and a half he started talking, but he still couldn't get whole words out. He was diagnosed at Medical College of Georgia with Verbal Dyspraxia. A lot of autistic kids get parts of words out but not the whole sound. If the word was "cow" he could say "ow" but he couldn't say the "c" sound.

He was in speech therapy until he was three, when they dropped his services. He was starting to come out of it. He overcame the Verbal Dyspraxia with about six months of speech therapy, then he started to stutter and he was diagnosed with Neurological Stuttering Disorder. In order to get words out he would bang his feet on the floor or close his eyes and push to get the words out, so he was in therapy for that. Now he's fine. He is super smart—it's wonderful. That's Connor. We were told by a couple of the most highly regarded autism specialists in the country that if we would have continued with Connor's vaccines he would have been where Joshua is today.

From my perspective, being a sibling of a child with autism is extremely difficult. I'd like to get Connor into a sibling support group even though he's so very young; he's very bright so I think he could benefit from talking about it. It's at least as hard on Connor, if not harder than it is on everybody else. When Joshua is being aggressive, he always hits Connor. He grew up with Joshua hitting and biting him. Joshua still bites. Joshua definitely isn't a pleasant kind of brother, a real brother to him. I talk to Connor about it. He knows the word autism; he knows about it, he knows about mercury. He tells me, "I don't like my brother. Why do I have to have a brother with autism?" Sometimes they play together, but for the most part they don't like each other. It's sad because Joshua is Connor's only brother. I can see the effect it has on Connor. I'm sure having a brother like Joshua changes Connor's whole outlook on life.

Many of the experiences we have together at home are very difficult and often traumatic. Today Joshua had a huge tantrum. He had a baseball game this evening. I brought him home and I told him, "You need to get ready right away," because it was an early game. He ignored me and kept playing. Next I said, "Joshua, your clothes are out here, if you don't get ready now it's going to be too late and we're not going to go." Well, of course, he waited too long and by the time he was ready to go I said, "I'm not taking you, the game has already started. To drive over there now would be ridiculous." He went wild screaming and yelling, "I want to go to my game!"

Consequently, Connor laughed at him, which is how he usually reacts. He's too young to express his emotions appropriately. When I try to tell him don't laugh, he just doesn't know how to deal with it. Of course, Connor's laughing makes Joshua angrier and Joshua will hit him. So I have to separate them. No matter how many times I've told Connor, "Joshua can't help it. The best thing you could do right now is step outside on the porch or go in your room; just keep clear of Joshua. I know it bothers you," his reaction is the same. He says, "I don't care." But I know it annoys him.

His way of dealing with it is to laugh because he doesn't know how else to handle it.

I wish I could do more for Joshua. There are a lot of innovative things out there people are doing now in addition to ABA and they are coming up with new methods all the time. If you get on the Internet people say that they really believe that the answer to this is catching it when they are very young. Fortunately we managed to save one and make significant improvements for the other.

Maurine's tip

- Remember, the longer you wait the more difficult it is to turn these kids around.

$$\text{\large ☙}$$

Stephanie, Meredith (5), and Nathalie (3)

Meredith is very happy, excitable, outgoing, and in constant motion. She needs to be entertained and always wants me to pay attention to her. Nathalie is quieter, though she loves music and singing. Nathalie likes to play outside by herself, but sometimes she will play with her sister. She reads a little and knows the alphabet.

With Meredith, at her two-year check-up the doctor asked me how many words she said. At that point she mostly said "Mama" and "Dada" and a couple of other words. The pediatrician thought that wasn't enough and contacted the school system in order to have them do some additional testing. Meredith was also self-abusive, with tantrums every 15 minutes or so for no apparent reason. The crying and screaming we attributed to colic as a baby continued as a toddler. After the preliminary consultation, my dad, who is a physician, said, "Why don't you have them check and evaluate her for something called autism?" To me it seemed like he suggested it out of the blue, but maybe it was more than a coincidence. I had her tested and quite a few red flags came up. Once they told me what the common characteristics of autism were I could see that she'd had them for some time. I had never heard or dealt with autism before and since she was my first child, I had figured that's what a normal two-year-old acts like.

On the other hand, when Nathalie came along we were looking for the same types of thing that had been problems for Meredith to be wrong with her. Everything appeared to be fine with Nathalie, but I learned that, with autism, a sibling has a 10 percent greater chance of being affected.

I decided to have Nathalie tested for my peace of mind, even though I knew there was nothing wrong with her. For Nathalie the tests came back with red flags too, just different ones than Meredith had. I was looking for Meredith-isms in Nathalie instead of looking for other symptoms of autism. Nathalie had no speech or eye contact but her manner was very calm. In fact, she would just go somewhere in her eyes and I couldn't get her to look at me or focus on anything. I couldn't get her out of wherever she went. Her diagnosis came as a bigger shock to me than Meredith's did because Nathalie didn't have the drastic issues we'd seen with Meredith.

For me, it's been a completely different experience with each girl and regardless of their diagnoses they have both turned out to be wonderful children. When each of the girls turned three, they began going to school. Quickly, Meredith went from a two-word vocabulary to reading us the newspaper. It's unbelievable how much the school has helped her. The teachers are truly amazing. School was the one thing she needed to turn herself around from what she was going through. Nathalie has been in school for only a few months and already she's using more words and interacting more appropriately with other people. She seems happier in general and more aware of what's going on in the world. Again, school was vital to her improvement.

Meredith had her re-evaluation this summer and it came back with such a low prognosis of autism that the state does not recognize her for funding any more. My husband and I went with our gut feeling and decided to send her to kindergarten instead of remaining in the preschool class for another year. She seemed to have grown so much emotionally and intellectually during summer school that we couldn't resist testing the waters with kindergarten. She has now spread her wings and flown to new heights that we never thought would be possible for her. Meredith has made friends, increased her sociability, and tried new adventures; exceeding our expectations in every way. Nathalie has a couple of the same teachers that Meredith had and they say Nathalie is on the same path as far as they can estimate. I'm thrilled with the progress they have both made—it is truly a dream come true.

Stephanie's tip

- Get some business cards printed up that provide some basic autism facts to educate people about what is going on, and pass them out if your child has a tantrum in a public place.

CR

Two professionals' perspectives: Claire Dees, SPECTRUM Co-Chairperson, and Cheryl A. Rhodes, licensed marriage and family therapist

Claire says: For the past eight years I have co-chaired the SPECTRUM autism support group in Gwinnett County, Georgia, and I also have a son with autism. Concurrent to our meetings, we sponsor a sibling group that is open to children aged 5–12 and lasts approximately an hour and a half per meeting. We also run a similar group that coincides with our Saturday respite program for parents. The Saturday meeting lasts six hours, which gives the kids additional time for making friends, doing special activities and one-on-one attention with the facilitator.

When siblings of autistic children have the opportunity to interact with other kids going through the same thing they realize they are not alone and that someone else understands the unusual issues they often face. It helps that they can laugh together about things others might not see the humor in. They have the chance to share with one another ideas and solutions to the unique problems they face.

During group meetings, siblings of children with autism express a variety of concerns. Most commonly among the younger children, these include a fear of the future, a sense of responsibility for the affected sibling, and a reluctance to leave their parents alone because they need to be around to help. Children who have aggressive siblings fear being physically hurt or injured by them. These children also convey anxiety when they believe their brother or sister will get better and they do not. Teenagers experience many of the same worries, in addition to embarrassment at their autistic sibling's behavior.

One of the most important things parents can do is let their typically developing children know that they are not responsible for the care of their brother or sister. They can also increase the sibling's sense of well-being by giving them individual attention away from home or while away from the autistic child.

Frequently, siblings of children with autism provide a unique insight into the situation—so as a parent it is especially important to listen to what these children are trying to communicate. For example, my daughter once corrected me and said I babied my autistic child too much and that my treating him and talking to him like he was an infant bothered her. I wasn't aware I was doing it until she brought it to my attention.

We must also ensure that our children are kept up to speed on what is happening with their autistic sibling. They need to be educated about autism at an age-appropriate level as well. During an especially difficult transition, where my son had a major medication change and my husband and I had to attend to him around the clock, my daughter had to ask me why people were bringing us meals. We had neglected to tell her what was going on even though she deserved to know. Keeping the lines of communication open, taking the time to do special things together, and getting your children involved in support groups (where available) will have a positive impact on the entire family.

Cheryl says: As facilitator of the SPECTRUM sibling group, I have the privilege to meet and learn from some awesome young people: boys and girls who are articulate, funny, sensitive, caring, and impacted in different ways by living with a brother or sister who has autism, Autism Spectrum Disorder or is on the spectrum. One young child explained why she came to the sibling group by stating, "We're autism." When an older child corrected her saying, "You mean your *brother* has autism," she insisted, "I know, but that means we're autism too." Everyone present agreed. A child's wisdom and simplicity underscores that all family members are affected by autism, not only the child with the diagnosis and his parents struggling to meet a variety of challenges, but his brothers and sisters too.

As Claire mentioned, the sibling group is held in conjunction with the monthly informational meeting for parents. Recently I was invited to speak to the parents about sibling concerns. Since the sibling group usually meets at the same time as the parent meeting, we had a sibling panel. Their comments were the highlight of the meeting and added an air of "authenticity" to the professional and research perspectives presented. This particular panel comprised five girls aged 7 through 12, but their comments and suggestions for parents were representative of common sibling concerns including family life, attention, privacy, increased responsibility, and future planning.

Additionally, their comments support research on the positive impact of growing up with a sibling with a disability such as opportunities to develop maturity, insight, tolerance, pride, loyalty, and empathy, as well as increased self-concept and social competence. For example, as much as they may complain about their sibling's behavior, if someone else teases or makes fun of their sibling they will quickly come to his defense. They say things like, "It's not right" and "I might have been a bully; now I've seen things differently in the world." Siblings demonstrate patience in trying to engage their siblings in play. One explained, "We have fun together. My brother lies down and makes me jump over him, over, and over, and over, and over." They're learning important lessons about respecting individual differences, fairness, and unconditional love by living them. Other comments include: "It opens your eyes to make you sensitive to different people," and "I wouldn't be the same if I had a regular brother. He teaches me a lot, too."

Talking with siblings about autism will not be a one-time discussion, but rather a dialogue that will continue and change over time. It's important to set the stage for open communication so that you will be prepared when the questions, concerns, challenges, or complaints come—and they will come! How you respond will either facilitate or inhibit communication. Take a deep breath, give your undivided attention, listen, and don't judge. Hear your child out—regardless of what you hear. Praise your child for sharing feelings and respect his point of view. Finally, elicit possible options or solutions.

Siblings may share strong feelings and it's especially important not to react defensively. Remember, they are trying to tell you how they feel and not trying to make you feel bad, although sometimes it may feel that way!

Cheryl's tips (comments from siblings in italics)

- Be honest. *When we ask a question and you don't know the answer, it's okay to tell us "I don't know."*

- Explain autism using words and concepts appropriate to their age and understanding. This is especially important to allay fears and misconceptions. Research suggests having accurate information about autism may increase the time siblings spend with their brother or sister with autism. *I knew my brother had autism because I heard my parents talking but then I asked them to tell me about it and now I know what it means.*

- Reassure siblings that they will be protected if their sibling is aggressive. *I try to help my brother but when he gets really rough I tell my mom or my dad and they take over. She said it's her job to help him, not mine, and that makes me feel safe.*

- Recognize the unique strengths and skills of siblings The special bond that exists between typical siblings is still evident when a sibling has autism. *We really understand each other. When my mom doesn't know what he's trying to say she'll ask me and usually I know what he wants.* On the other hand, siblings have a need to be valued and appreciated for who they are, not what they do. *I'm not any different than a normal kid [because my sibling has autism]. I'm just me.*

- Respect siblings' needs for privacy, private time with parents, and time with friends. Our panel talked about wanting an "autism-free zone," a place where they could work on projects, do their homework, or play games with friends or family without their sibling with autism. Siblings understand that parents can't always be available, yet they really appreciated having special time with a parent (or grandparent) and being heard when they asked for attention. They also appreciated their parents' understanding when they chose to spend time at the home of friends (instead of their own). *When I tried to get my mom's attention by slamming my door it didn't work, but then I tried saying, "Mom, I need some attention" it actually worked! My mom said she knows why I like to spend so much time at my best friend's house and even joked that sometimes she wishes she could come with me.*

- Teach siblings how to engage their sibling with autism in simple games. *He doesn't do the playing technically; I do something and he'll imitate me. When I play with my brother we do the things he likes to do.*

- Demonstrate fairness for siblings. *I know my brother gets away with things that I wouldn't because he can't help it, but I get to do things he's not allowed to do too.*

- Give siblings access to sibling groups and age-appropriate literature. Many state and local autism groups sponsor sibling groups, workshops, and conferences. Information is available in print and on websites. There are numerous books written by adult siblings, and fiction containing autism themes for siblings of various ages from the very young to young adult. The Sibling Support Project of the Association for Retarded Citizens (Arc) of the United States sponsors Sibshops, SibNet, SibKids, and publications for parents, professionals, and children (www.thearc.org/siblingsupport).

- Help children explain their sibling's disability to friends and classmates. *At first I didn't know how to explain to my friends some of the weird things my brother does, but I talked about it with my mom and we figured out what to say.*

- Make plans for the future. Siblings are aware that, to some extent, they will be involved in caring for their sibling with autism. *I was worried about what would happen to my brother and who will take care of him, but my parents told me not to worry because they will make a plan for the future. I'll go to college while my parents try to get him into a good place.*

- Make time to laugh and have fun as a family. Humor definitely helps get us through the tough times.

- Don't worry every time you hear, "It's not fair!" Jealousy and competition between siblings is universal, and time and attention do not equal love. As one sibling summed it up: *He brings us together more because we're in it as a family.*

A consultant and trainer with over 30 years of professional experience, Cheryl is a proud parent of three young adults aged 17, 19, and 22, including a daughter with multiple disabilities, who are her greatest teachers.

Cheryl can be contacted at rhodcan@bellsouth.net.

SOMETHING TO TALK ABOUT

1. How do the reactions of older/younger siblings differ in regard to their sibling on the spectrum?

2. What kinds of complaints do you hear most frequently from your child's siblings in regard to their behavior? What could you do to address/alleviate these complaints?

3. What special considerations might you give to the sibling not affected with autism?

4. Why do you think many older siblings of children with autism are described as "perfect" children?

5. What are some things you can do to cope with the stress of having more than one child on the spectrum?

6. How can you foster a better relationship between your child with autism and his siblings?

7. What are some common problems faced by children who have siblings with autism?

REFLECTION ACTIVITY

Sit down with your child and discuss the "Aunt Blabby" questions found at www.autism.org. Find out if he or she has any questions to send to "Aunt Blabby."

6.

You Are What You Eat: Parents Speak Out on Diet and Food

Chuck and Kyle (9)

We're working on trying to get Kyle more active because his diet is so poor and he is severely overweight for his age. It's hard to get him to exercise, and hard for us as well. We've tried to get him to do sit-ups, but that involves me holding his feet down and my wife pushing him back and forth. By the time we're finished, all of us end up getting a workout! He can't swim yet, but he does like to walk around in the pool.

Kyle has some coordination issues. He's into bicycling right now, so I purchased a bicycle for him. He uses footbrakes with no problem, but since he's such a big boy he needs an adult-sized bike. Fortunately, they still make bikes like that, but he still needs training wheels. The funny part is the bicycle was only $100, but the training wheels were $80. If I could only teach him how to balance—but you can't teach someone balance if they can't feel it. That's basically the only form of exercise he gets other than bouncing on the trampoline, and that is sporadic.

Pizza is the staple of Kyle's diet. We attempted the gluten-free, casein-free (GFCF) diet but found that it is very difficult to stay away from foods that do not have wheat or cheese in them. If you want to go to a restaurant to eat, it is virtually impossible to stay away from those ingredients. The doctor explained to us that when these foods leak through the digestive system it creates opiates to the brain. In turn, the increased level of opiates contributes to the weird behaviors and insensitivity to pain often associated with autism. Our doctor also said that Kyle is probably so seriously addicted to the heightened opiate production that he couldn't physically tolerate the diet unless we checked him into the hospital to go through physiological withdrawal in a monitored setting. It is going to take years for us to get him on to any form of that diet. Unfortunately, when we experimented with it, we went cold turkey; that was when he figured out how to become self-abusive and beat his head into the wall. I learned that that response is a typical withdrawal effect. He was violent and beating himself up in a manner similar to what a drug addict would experience during withdrawal from heroin.

Obviously, completely removing milk and wheat products from Kyle's diet was a mistake on our part, so now we're trying to do it gradually. The other problem we've run into with the diet is there seems to be nothing that is gluten-free that satisfies his hunger. Most of the filling foods Kyle likes are wheat based, like pizza or spaghetti. Popcorn seems to be an okay choice, but the chips he likes are made of wheat. Filling foods aren't on the diet, but that's the only way he'll stop being hungry. Many of the things that are on the diet, such as chicken and broccoli, we have to liquefy in the food processor because he doesn't like the texture and they become the equivalent of mush. He gets other foods, just not in their original form. We keep trying though.

Chuck's tips

- Be careful when using information you find on the web. The treatment that is right for one child might be the absolute worst thing for your child.

- Approach each individual problem that your child displays separately rather than trying to attack autism as a whole.

⁓

Corinne and C.J. (12)

Frequently, the topic of food tends to come up when parents of children with developmental disorders get together. Due to C.J.'s additional diagnosis of cystic fibrosis and the need for a certain amount of calories per day, the GFCF diet is not an option for us. Accordingly, C.J. has created his own ultra-specific breakfast regimen. For the past two years, almost every day he has eaten two bowls of Fruit Loops cereal with just enough milk so that the cereal reaches the top of the sides of the bowl. When they are available, he will also add a Limited Edition Dr. Seuss Pop Tart with the edges peeled off. C.J. says, "Why bother, there's no filling and no frosting!" His other morning food option consists of a plate of pre-made, frozen pancakes heated for exactly 48 seconds in the microwave. Of course, they have to be placed in a certain orientation and can only be the kind in a blue box. He places a small ovenproof cup of pure maple syrup in the middle of the pancake formation. On a whim, one day I bought a different brand of pancakes, but I think they are still in the freezer.

Sometimes I worry because C.J. is so particular about what he eats. For instance, this month he is attending summer camp, and I was really worried if he would get enough calories. In addition to his other food routines, he eats very little meat. When he does occasionally try some, it must be boneless, without seasoning, and definitely not brown. A few days after he arrived at camp, I received a letter in the mail from him. The entire letter was about the meal his first night at camp; he ate five pieces of fried chicken, *on the bone!* He was so excited. I cried when I read that. After finishing the letter, I said to myself, "He's away at camp, on his own, and he's not going to starve. C.J. is going to be all right!"

ை

Julie and Jake (7)

The minute Jake was born I fell in love with him instantly. He was a beautiful baby with blonde hair and bright blue eyes. Not unlike his older sister Stephanie, Jake was an easy baby. He slept through the night soon after we brought him home, and he was always smiling and happy. He rarely got sick during his first year of life. I did notice some differences between him the other two children, especially where food was concerned. I nursed him for six months and then weaned him onto formula. At nine months old, the only solid foods he would eat were yogurt and crackers. Jake would spit out all other baby food. Other than that, life seemed normal.

At his first-year check-up, Jake had just received a clean bill of health when the doctor said it was time to introduce "whole milk." That was the beginning of our nightmare. Within weeks of starting him on cows' milk, Jake developed chronic colds and ear and sinus infections, which required many doses of antibiotics to treat. This went on for about a year. I kept asking the pediatrician if it was the milk causing the problems, and she stated, "I don't know, but you could try removing it." I worried about him getting enough calcium, so I didn't. If only I were smarter back then. His mood changed and he drooled constantly. He started walking on his tiptoes, and his words became more like babble. After 18 months, he was no longer my sweet happy baby. Jake became very aggressive by biting, kicking, and scratching anyone he came in contact with. He also stopped calling me "Mama" at that point. I knew something wasn't right!

Jake desperately craved milk and would consume eight bottles a day, rarely eating anything else. By this time, my husband's job had relocated us to Seattle. We seldom left the house with Jake because of the meltdowns and his inability to control himself. He could not be around other children because he would hurt them. I was pleading with my pediatric group to help me find out what was wrong with Jake, explaining repeatedly to the doctors that he didn't understand what I was saying and that I could not communicate with him. They just kept giving me parent help books. (Just so you know, I had a book-burning party several years later, and it felt wonderful!)

We had been living in Seattle eight months, and it was Christmas time. My husband Bill asked me what I wanted for Christmas, but all I could do was break down and cry. Tearfully, I told him I wanted to go home to Ohio and find a doctor who could help Jake. Seeing my desperation, Bill agreed and once again we began making preparations for the cross-country move.

While packing, I came across an article in *Parents Magazine*, by Karen Serrousi. She described her son's symptoms and the diet she used to help him. To my surprise, Jake had the exact same symptoms as her son's: speech delay, drooling, tantrums, and head dragging. The diagnosis was autism! A nauseating feeling came over me as I realized, "Oh my, Jake is autistic." To this day, I still have that wadded, crinkled article in my files.

When we got back to Ohio, we saw Jake's former pediatrician who was also his doctor at birth. The last time she had seen him, he was three months old. She was upset by the fact that his symptoms had not been checked into further by professionals. She recommended hearing, speech, blood, urine, and gastrointestinal (GI) testing. I also showed her the Serrousi article, at which she gasped, "Jake is not autistic!"

Our pediatrician suggested a special educational preschool here in Columbus for speech and learning disabled children. It was very costly, but we were told it was "the best." I remember being a nervous wreck on the first day. Of course, I battled him to sit in his car seat and, sure enough, he had a meltdown, threw his head against the table and busted his lip open. The other children were somewhat traumatized by this bloody episode, and the staff later told me they weren't sure what to do with Jake. I had heard about children being institutionalized for this kind of behavior, but I couldn't bear to think about it.

On the morning of Jake's third birthday, I read an article in the newspaper about an autism group, which included information on a local Defeat Autism Now (DAN) physician. The biomedical approach was something I wanted to try. We immediately scheduled an appointment with the DAN doctor; however, there was a three-month wait before we could get in to see him.

At this point, my daily regime went something like this… I got up extra early to have my morning coffee and mentally prepare myself for the crazy day ahead. I would also ask God to help me through the day and give me strength each day. Jake would wake up with a scream, and then he would usually cry once he woke up until I went into his room to console him. The only way he would eat something was if it was on the floor in a bowl, because he couldn't sit at a table. He would drink milk as well. Seven or eight times a day I'd chase him around the house in order to change his soiled diaper; if I didn't, his bottom would have a blistered rash in no time. Jake didn't have any speech and just babbled at the time. I sometimes put a hat on him to wear throughout the day because he had a tendency to drag his head across the floor. He rarely played with toys and would throw a fit if I tried to read him a book. He hated the car seat, and every trip was a struggle. Our little Jake would scream uncontrollably if I put him in the car.

It was difficult to take Jake anywhere. He was a very busy fellow and very hyperactive. He was everywhere and climbed hazardously onto everything. We had to install locks on the doors so he wouldn't escape and run out in the street.

I remember being very physically and emotionally exhausted by dinnertime. My daughter, who was four years old at the time, struggled with Jake's violent tantrums and would actually mimic the behaviors for attention. It was difficult to explain to her, "It's okay for him, but not okay for you." Most of the time, my husband reverted to his office for peace and quiet. Late at night, I would secretly go out to the garage, sob, and smoke a cigarette. This became my coping mechanism. If there was a definition of "dysfunctional family" in a book, our picture could have been next to it. It was a very painful time for us, and it sucked the life right out of me.

Frustrated and grieving, I referred back to the newspaper article and stumbled across a website address for a company called Kirkman Labs. I contacted their customer service department and explained my dilemma with Jake. The representative took the time to explain the GFCF diet and other helpful supplements she felt would be appropriate. At this point, I was desperate and had nothing to lose. I planned ahead, did some more research, and within three days of initiating the dietary changes, a miracle happened.

It was morning, and I was standing in the kitchen as usual when I heard a little pitter-patter of footsteps coming downstairs. I assumed it was my daughter Stephanie who was five at the time. To my surprise, it was Jake. He sat down at the table and said the words, "I eat, Mommy." I was in such total shock that my knees gave out. When I pulled myself off the floor, tears of joy streaming down my face, I scrambled to find him something to eat.

From that point on, Jake has only continued to progress. Shortly thereafter he started to speak in short sentences, and he also understood how to go potty within a week. His frequent wild meltdowns were reduced to only two a day. Jake was able to stay in his preschool, but the best part of it all was that he had called me Mommy!

Eventually we saw the DAN doctor, who confirmed that Jake did indeed have low-functioning autism. However, it was a local nutritionist here in town who made a world of difference for Jake. A chiropractor for 20 years, he had decided to branch out and use his background in nutrition to help those people who had nowhere else to turn. I know an angel brought us together. We adhered to his suggestions for a strict program of diet, supplements, and various treatments. With that, Jake kept improving.

In the meantime, we were spending about $1800 a month out of pocket on food and other interventions, and were headed to financial devastation. Like many other moms, I was unable to work and keep up with Jake's appointments, not to mention all his food preparation. My husband Bill was all for the treatments, but the cost did put a lot of strain on the family finances, as well as our marriage. We ended up selling our house and moved into a rental for two years while we continued working toward getting Jake well.

Over the next few years, we had our ups and downs. Jake showed some promising steps forward only to spiral back down. When Jake was four years old he had five foods he would eat on a regular basis. I remember excitedly calling my husband at the office to tell him that Jake tried jello today, but only reached his voicemail. Later, when Bill called me back, he was thrilled to hear the news but was upset I hadn't interrupted his meeting to tell him. He said, "That is so important, you please interrupt my meeting the next time!" I could imagine what his employees would have thought about that one. We chuckle thinking back to those times. What I once considered to be a curse with Jake turned out to be a true blessing.

Another positive outcome of having a child with autism is that our entire family is healthier. A few months after starting Jake's initial diet, I decided to go on it with him. Jake was beginning to realize that his food was different than ours so I did what any good parent would do, and I dieted along with him. Honestly, I have never felt better in my life. I never knew that I was lactose intolerant! My mental clarity improved, and at 40 years old, my adult acne cleared up. I don't believe I would have experienced those changes if it weren't for Jake. Even my daughter had some problems that were eliminated by the changes in our diet.

In the last few years, I have attended many conferences and seminars on autism and related disorders. I keep learning more and more. I even went back to school and obtained my nutrition certification so I could teach some of these methods to other parents who have an autistic child. I am now a state representative for Unlocking Autism and correspond weekly with parents of newly diagnosed children.

When I tell people that Jake had an autistic diagnosis at one point, they don't believe me because he appears so typical. He attends first grade in a regular classroom, played on a basketball team this past winter, and is thriving in his drama class. Jake is very comical, and he loves to perform and make people happy. I know we will be beaming ear to ear at his first performance. I was told several years ago to never expect this from Jake.

As a family, we no longer place a high priority on materialistic things and we have managed to pull ourselves out of financial ruin. We focus on health and family instead. Guess what? Our picture is no longer on the dysfunctional list. It took hard work, sacrifice, and teamwork to get Jake where he is today.

Julie's tips

- I was told on three separate occasions by three different professionals that I needed counseling for thinking I could erase my son's autism label. Remember, while not every child will improve to what is considered "normal," there is hope for a better quality of life for all children.

- Focus on "intensity and consistency," like Joni Jones, community advocate and educator (www.autism-resources.net) says. I would like to add two more to that: "read and research."

CR

Sonya and Isaiah (4)

When Isaiah was about two years old we began to notice something was wrong. He wasn't responding. We had suspected that something had happened to Isaiah during his last set of immunizations. We moved from the city where we were living to where we are now when Isaiah was just 15 or 16 months old. Our pediatrician was still in the old city, and we were just in the process of getting settled down in the house, so he was about 20 months old by the time we actually took him back to get his vaccinations.

Within a few weeks, we started noticing these strange behaviors, but I didn't think about it until much later. He had tantrums that got progressively worse. He was flapping his hands and lining up his cars. We prayed for help to know what to do. We took him to a school for the deaf to have him tested, but nothing was wrong with his hearing. We had Isaiah evaluated by another doctor and began occupational therapy two months before he was officially diagnosed with autism.

One evening, I attended a meeting of the women's auxiliary at our church, and the topic was health and nutrition. The doctor who presented the information was a DAN doctor from Autism Now. I called him the next day and we set up an appointment. He saw Isaiah two or three times before he moved practice to Louisiana. The doctor who took his place wasn't a DAN doctor, and we didn't feel comfortable going back. Since then, we just feel blessed that we had that opportunity to be introduced to that methodology. When we changed Isaiah's diet according to the first doctor's recommendations, the tantrums stopped *immediately*. I thought, "This is do-able!" Not only did the tantrums decrease, but his hyperactivity was reduced, and he became much calmer in general. The other therapies have made a substantial difference, too.

We have tried a variety of alternative methods to reduce autism-related behaviors—Isaiah has never been on any type of medication. Currently, we are taking him to see a nurse in Atlanta who has many years of experience working with autistic children. The nurse performed a biophysical assessment on Isaiah. The assessment used acupuncture sites on his body and was non-invasive.

The nurse was able to perform this bioenergetics assessment with this wand that looks like an ink pen. Isaiah had to hold the wand in his right hand and she would touch acupuncture sites in his left hand with the wand, which registered corresponding data on the computer. She went through the different systems in the body to see if anything was out of balance. Then she went back and attempted to pinpoint the cause of any irregularities. The whole process took about an hour, including receiving the results. Everything was done right there in her office, and she didn't even have to draw any blood. When the assessment was complete, she informed us that Isaiah had metal poisoning from mercury, lead, and aluminum. Following the assessment, Isaiah went through a process called chelation therapy to remove the metals. At his last follow-up, he didn't have any more of the heavy metals in his system.

Also, Isaiah has a "leaky gut" and a yeast overgrowth that is common in a lot of kids with autism. One book I read talked about how many children with autism can't digest foods with gluten and casein protein. The undigested protein travels to the brain through their blood and causes a lot of problems or changes in their body. Think about a packet of yeast—when you add sugar and warm water, it bubbles up. When a child has a yeast overgrowth and you give him sugar, you get the same result. Due to the yeast overgrowth, he got a leaky gut. The yeast was eating away at the lining of his stomach. Can you imagine that? That's what was happening with his stomach. The lining of his stomach was thinning out due to the yeast overgrowth, so practically nothing he was eating was being digested properly. When we took him to have the blood test to check for food allergies, a leaky gut was one of the diagnoses. It confirmed what we already knew.

Back when we saw the DAN doctor, he gave us some suppositories that could be used for a child with a yeast overgrowth. We gave Isaiah these suppositories at night for 14 days and also put him on a low-sugar diet to help with yeast control. He still has some yeast overgrowth, but it's certainly not to the extent it used to be. Before, it was out of control, and now it's not that way. We just have to continue to treat it with acidophilus, which you can get from the health food store. It comes in capsule form, and it's simply the good bacteria that your body needs to fight off the bad bacteria. So now it's under control, but we still have to watch and not give him a whole lot of sugar. He's on a diet that doesn't contain sugar anyway, but he still gets natural sugar in fruit and in juices. We have to dilute that and make sure that we don't give him too much, and we continue to see progress.

Now Isaiah is back to where he understands and follows commands, and we can tell him, "Isaiah turn off the light," and he'll turn the light off, or "Close the door," and he'll close the door. He likes going to school. He's in a special pre-K class for five days a week. He will say a few words, like "bye-bye," "hi," and "car." He still loves to play with cars, but he doesn't line them up like he used to. His comprehension has improved. Mentally, now we feel like he's with us. He tries to say a lot more words, and he's using some sign language.

In many respects, Isaiah has made a lot of progress. We remain open to trying different things with his diet. Now he's at a point where he can't have white flour, but he can have whole wheat. He can also have oats, whereas before he couldn't have any type of grain. He can have rice milk and certain cheeses like mozzarella and parmesan, so we have more options for meals.

One of the biggest changes has been for the family socially. We used to go out for dinner a lot. The entire family has made dietary changes, and we have all seen a difference. It helped my husband's cholesterol, and he and I have both lost weight because we're eating healthier. We don't go out to eat because almost all the food in restaurants has some type of additive or preservative that may hurt Isaiah. We just do a lot of things at home. We don't use a lot of processed foods either. So I think, dietary and nutrition-wise, it's helped a lot.

Otherwise, our extended family has become closer because of Isaiah. His aunts and uncles and grandparents are now learning more about autism, and are becoming more involved. Last year we participated in an autism walk in Atlanta. We had a group of friends and family called "Team Isaiah," and even though it rained that morning, we still had 20 people show up from our team to walk. Socially, we still go out to family gatherings, but we always have to take food with us. Some people may think that's a big inconvenience, but I don't look at it that way. I see the extra effort as doing what it takes to help my child. I'm just grateful and blessed that I'm a stay-home mom and I have the time to do it. If I had to go out there and work, I don't know if I could put all this energy and effort into doing what I'm doing as far as the diet goes.

There is a certain degree of challenge that our diet brings. For instance, we have to make our own chicken nuggets. On this diet we can't go to McDonald's and get chicken nuggets any more. Some people think I'm just crazy, but when I go to the health food store or the farmers' market and I see something I can use I just get so excited: "Yea! I can use this." I found this special coating for the chicken nuggets. We tried it and it was so good— they were delicious. Now we can have chicken nuggets again. We make it fun. I don't think our other kids feel deprived of anything. Of course, there are certain things, like regular ice cream, that we don't have in the house, but there is always Rice Dream.

We've also experimented with incorporating principles of the Feingold program into our dietary regimen, which is supposed to be helpful for people with ADHD, ADD, and autism. Through that process we discovered Isaiah has sensitivities to tomato products. A while ago, he was at school and was running around in circles (he doesn't do that normally), so his teacher called me from school and said, "Isaiah's been into something." She knows he's on a special diet. I realized the night before I had made spaghetti with rice noodles, and the sauce had tomatoes in it. We had also had something with tomatoes the previous day. I recalled reading something about kids being allergic to tomatoes and citrus, and made the connection to his behavior. We waited maybe a month and gave him spaghetti one night, and the next day he was acting the same way he did that day at school. So I am learning some new things with the Feingold program that can improve things for Isaiah.

Keenan, our middle child, and I will go out together sometimes, and we'll just get a slice of pizza together. That's something we just can't do as a family. I try to make sure Keenan doesn't feel like he's being punished because he doesn't get to eat the things his friends do. I think he appreciates that one-on-one time, too. We'll go into Sam's and get a slice of pizza right there in the deli and hang out together. Like I said, we make it work.

Sonya's tips

- Don't get overwhelmed by the big picture. Take it one day at a time.

- Be resourceful. Be an advocate for your child. Be available and be willing to go out there and do your own homework, and be willing to try different things.

- Don't just take what the doctor says and go. If I had just listened to the first doctor, I'd feel hopeless. There was a doctor who just didn't give me any hope. You have to take it with a grain of salt and find resources that can help.

☙

Susan and Mark (10)

Mark is very particular about his foods…I'm not sure how much is behavior related and how much is intrinsic. Certain foods really, sincerely make him gag and almost throw up. Chicken nuggets are limited to one particular brand; even McDonald's won't do, because to him chicken nuggets are supposed to be one way and one way only. He'll eat toast, but only white. Bagels—don't cut or toast them, and don't even think of putting anything on them, and he'll eat a dozen. We'll sit and feed him bite-by-bite scrambled eggs to earn the toast. French fries are a definite "to die for," and we can get him to try new foods and/or eat healthy foods by making him eat them to "earn" the fries. Some foods he will try to eat, like ham to earn the fries, but you can tell he just can't make himself do it. Getting him to eat almost any meat or protein in any form is work. Oddly enough, he likes tuna salad. Thankfully, he eats broccoli too, and we've had it every night for about eight years now.

When Mark was younger, we could not vary our mealtime at all, but now he is more flexible. He went through a milk-only and juice-only phase, but for the past three years he has drunk only water with ice from a clear or white glass, or water from a fountain. Most foods that he does eat take a lot of encouragement. Mark is definitely the carbohydrate-, wheat-seeking boy. On vacation, I was helping my daughter get ice cream while Mark appeared content. I only took my eyes off him for two minutes and returned to find him chowing down on an entire loaf of French bread—he was in heaven.

CR

A professional's perspective: Pattie Pilling, Registered Nurse, Psychiatry and Pediatrics

Think about the autistic body as if it were a fire; if you take away things like gluten and casein you are not continually adding fuel to the fire. The fire is still there, but it is not going to get any bigger—the flames will dissipate. By changing diet you are not going to eliminate autism since it interferes with physical, behavioral, and emotional aspects of development. However, many of the erratic symptoms will be reduced by adhering to a specific nutritional regimen.

My son Nathan has autism. After only a few weeks of beginning the GFCF diet we began to see changes. Positive effects, such as longer attention span, improved interactive communication, increased speech and language, and healthier sleeping patterns occur in many children after beginning the diet, and we experienced similar results. We began the nutritional changes only after our son was well established in various other interventions, so we know it was the diet that made the difference. The process involves so much more than putting your child on a diet, but I can say from first-hand experience that the results are worth it.

One of the main reasons dietary interventions do not work is that you have to be conscientious about what your child eats. This is not always the easiest of tasks. No more Kraft dinner. No more pizzas. No more bread. As we know it, that is—there are great alternatives for all these products. With a little perseverance it becomes second nature. Even though gluten and casein are in many of the products purchased in supermarkets, we are able to shop there and buy most of what we need. We have just had to become avid label readers!

A lifestyle change is involved. Many parents mistakenly assume this change has to occur overnight, which is an option, but for most families a more gradual transition is preferred. Some parents choose to remove the wheat first, others choose the dairy, and still others begin with eliminating the products from a certain meal each day. I encourage the families I consult with to find out what works best for them and then do it.

Another factor that impacts the success of nutritional interventions is the order in which they are initiated. Sometimes families will begin supplementation prior to removing gluten and casein from the diet. They spend a lot of money but are disappointed when nothing happens. Basically, this method is like taking a diet pill every morning but then stopping at McDonald's every day for lunch—intentions are good, but it's just not going to work. By doing things in that order you are still adding fuel to the fire; the harmful elements have not been removed.

Some families jump into the fire too quickly and end up getting burned out. For the optimal chance of success, I recommend giving the GFCF diet a minimum of three months' concerted effort before deciding it is not right for your child. Positive professional support and guidance during the early months is crucial because it involves a new way of looking at things. The impulse is to find the easy way or give up when we don't see immediate results—so keep it simple, as simple as you possibly can. Our families see such a difference in their children and in their family's lives that they are willing to do whatever is necessary.

I would urge you to further investigate this road of nutrition (you will find a list of recommended reading in Appendix D). No amount of therapy can replace it; it only makes therapy more helpful. Proper nutrition, including supplementation, is vital for our children to lead as normal lives as possible.

To contact Pattie for further information, go to www.autismnutrition.com.

SOMETHING TO TALK ABOUT

1. What are some of the benefits typically seen when dietary changes are made?

2. What are some of the drawbacks and more difficult aspects of the GFCF diet?

3.   What types of children are most likely to benefit from the GFCF diet?

4.   Why do some children report drastic improvements/dramatic reactions following dietary changes while others see few results, or none?

5.   How do you feel a radical change in diet will impact your family's life?

6.   What are the best sources of information when considering dietary changes for a child with autism?

REFLECTION ACTIVITY

We all know there is a definite relationship between food and physiology. Over the next three days, take stock of what you are eating and keep a food journal. Note any changes in your behavior or mood. Also look at the consequences of your food choices—how did your reactions to others (including spouse, children, and co-workers) vary according to your eating habits? Make a resolution to nourish your body as well as your soul.

7

Take a Stand: Advocacy, Community Involvement, and Awareness Activities

Anne and Alex (11)

As an educator and as a parent, I am very interested in the No Child Left Behind Act passed by the United States Government, which has in reality left every special education student behind. I represented our school district in a forum at our state capitol a few years ago when the undersecretary of the Secretary of Education came to make a presentation about No Child Left Behind. After the prepared speech, she fielded some questions from the audience. I said, "I don't understand how we can call this 'No Child Left Behind' when special education students are not part of this bill." As I uttered the last word the audience of teachers began applauding wildly. I thought, "Oh my God, I am so fired."

The speaker kept insisting that they were indeed included, just not in this particular bill. I went on to say, "If they are not represented in this bill, and it's called 'No Child Left Behind' then you are, in fact, leaving them behind." She never got my point. After the meeting I was escorted to the stage by the state Department of Education's assistant where they tried in vain to explain it to me. I must be a really defiant person because I won't sit there and accept an insufficient explanation any more. That all came from having to deal with the system and learn on my own what the law says.

Another time I spoke out was when our school system was going to switch to all-day kindergarten in my hometown. The school board was hosting a big, open meeting, and we decided to attend because Alex would be in that class. My husband Allen and I went to listen to what they planned on doing, but we made a decision beforehand not to say anything about Alex's diagnosis. We were simply putting our two cents in about how we felt about him going to school all day. The next week, when the local newspaper covered the story, they quoted me, but on top of that they said that I worked in a school district 15 miles away and that my son had autism. Right there in black and white for everyone to see was my son's diagnosis. I thought, "This cannot be legal." We didn't say anything about Alex's diagnosis that night. We were very guarded about what we said about Alex.

Later that day, when I spoke with the editor, he told me that they certainly were entitled to print that information and they were protected by law. According to him, it definitely was not a problem. I couldn't believe it. How could it possibly be all right to throw his diagnosis out for the whole world to see when there are so many laws to protect medical records from being shared with a third party? We hadn't even told some of our friends. I called the Office of Advocacy because I was so upset. Regrettably, the Advocacy people agreed with the newspaper. The editor was right; if at least one person in the community knew, then it was a matter of public knowledge. Fortunately, the editor is now much more sensitive about what he prints. Now, if you go to a public meeting and you're the parent of a special needs child, he doesn't put your name or the student's name in the article. Perhaps something like this wouldn't matter in a bigger city, but privacy is important when you live among a very small population.

Anne's tips

- Be aware when you are in the public eye that your child could potentially be affected.

- Learn about your child's rights. If you feel that his rights have been infringed on, take a stand. It may not help the current situation, but it might make a difference for your child or another child in the future.

CR

Barbie and John Matthew (10)

The main reason why I co-founded the Asperger's Syndrome/High Functioning Autism Support Group in Las Vegas was the treatment we received by the doctor who diagnosed John Matthew. He pretty much said, "Here's the diagnosis. Have a nice day!" I didn't have a clue what to do. My son had this lifelong disability, and I had no idea how to help even now that I knew what he had.

After overcoming the initial heartache of being the parent of a child with Asperger's Syndrome, I felt totally helpless. Following months of searching, we found a professional who had just graduated from medical school and was starting to do work with social skills and Asperger's Syndrome. John Matthew was in her very first social skills group. About a year and a half later, another parent in the social skills group, Danielle, and I decided that we ought to start a support group for parents so they wouldn't have to go through what we went through. Her story is similar to mine: she didn't know what to do or who to call after her daughter was diagnosed. I'm sure there were a couple of agencies in town we could have called for help, but if you don't know who they are, it's as good as if they didn't exist at all.

In 2002, when we started the support group, there were ten parents at the first meeting. Three years later, there are over 200 members in the group, and we get calls for assistance daily. During the third month of the group, we had a program called "Meet the Professionals." A local psychiatrist, occupational therapist, speech therapist, and a representative from an advocacy group here in Nevada called Parents Educating Parents (specializing in legal issues in the schools, Applied Behavioral Analysis (ABA) workshops, etc.) each spoke briefly about the services they could offer. After a panel discussion, each of the professionals had their own table where parents could ask more questions and set up appointments. It was wonderful!

Generally, about three-quarters of our meetings are spent with parents just talking to each other, but approximately four times a year we have information sessions. Everything is free. I still get as much out of it as the new parents do—we all have our ups and downs. One of the best parts is being around parents who understand what you are going through. Unless you talk to other families and ask, "What are you doing?" or "Have you ever tried this?" you will miss out on a lot of wonderful things that there are available.

Recently, we hosted our Second Annual Asperger's Picnic to commemorate Autism Awareness Month (April) with over 220 people in attendance. The picnic is great because it gives the kids a chance to get to know each other. All the parents know each other already, but the kids have limited opportunities to interact. About a year ago, we sent out an email to our members that basically said if you want your kid to meet other kids in our support group, send us their name, age, and the area of town you live in, and describe your kid's interests. From that we made a huge contact list, and I compiled it and gave it to the parents who participated. There were kids on the list from as young as three to the oldest who was in his early twenties.

Additionally, a couple of years ago, I called one of the local recreational programs in town that has a soccer program and asked if they had anything for children with higher-functioning disabilities. I knew there were places for kids with Down's Syndrome and other disabilities, but there didn't seem to be anything for kids that are intelligent but just don't fit in socially. Our kids want to be part of the crowd but aren't accepted. The director of this particular organization said, "I've always wanted to do something like this. Why don't you get about 20 of your parents together who want their kids to participate, and we'll play soccer, and I will be the coach." We ended up with ten kids on each team (all Asperger's), and the organization paid for everything from uniforms to soccer league fees to trophies at the end of the season.

The coach researched and found out as much as he could about Asperger's Syndrome. He came to one of our support group meetings and listened to parents' concerns with regard to recreational activities, and set up the program accordingly. We had a 30-minute practice before each game, so everything was on the same day. He scheduled the games in the late morning because he knew the kids would be tired in the afternoon. If the kids started to melt down on the field, they were just stepped over—no big deal. If the kids were getting stressed out, the coach gave them an extra break. Parents brought three sets of snacks just in case. When necessary everyone stopped and ate oranges and drank juice. We'd take a five-minute break and then everyone would go back out ready to continue. Parents could be on the field to assist but the goal was to have no parents on the field at the end of seven weeks. By the fifth week, there wasn't a single parent out there. We didn't keep score. All the kids ran and participated. Everyone cheered for both sides when they scored. Whenever they played, there wasn't a dry eye in the bleachers. The parents weren't stressed out because they were afraid the kids weren't good enough. The kids were finally doing something they weren't being judged negatively for and having the time of their lives.

Barbie's tip

- Join a support group. If there's not one in your area, start one (see Appendix C).

☙

Dolly

My job as a certified skills trainer allows me to work as a one-on-one aide with children on the spectrum. I serve mainly preschool-aged non-verbal children. While many of the children have challenges with language, they can communicate in other ways. I have used sign language with some kids I've worked with, and they pick that up in various degrees depending on what level of the spectrum they are on. I am also a guardian *ad litem* for the court system working with kids in foster care where I specialize in working with disabled children. A friend of mine got me involved with autistic children about five years ago. I love being with them and seeing any progression, even if it's very little, because to me, every step forward is a big deal.

Basically, I am a child-advocate for the underdog and for the child who slips through the cracks in the court system. Often, when I get a case, the children have never had access to the services they should have received in order to gain more sociability. I become their voice. In other words, I am a civil rights advocate for disabled children's rights. I work with the legislators locally here in Hawaii, and I'm very involved with Individuals with Disabilities Education Act (IDEA) legislation. That's my specialty. People within the autism community know me, so I get a lot of calls.

Services here in Hawaii are adequate, but you have to fight to get anything. I became involved with the Autism Society of Hawaii to promote awareness because parents with a newly diagnosed child don't know where to go or where to start. We have meetings once a month and we send out newsletters in addition to having special programs, speakers, and training. We help the parents as much as we can, but the services a child is entitled to depend on the diagnosis. A dual diagnosis makes it trickier—the children have to have the autism diagnosed to get proper services. If they just have "autistic mannerisms" they're not going to get the services that a child labeled autistic would receive.

One of the most common setbacks for families that I have seen is not getting a diagnosis as soon as possible. Early Intervention lays the groundwork for other progress. The earlier the diagnosis is given, the more services a child is likely to receive. Many parents are in denial or figure that the child is slower than normal and will grow out of it on their own, and end up waiting until it is too late. Actually, it's never too late to start treatment, but frequently earlier intervention is met with better results. Fortunately, now that there is so much more awareness and education concerning autism, doctors are able to diagnose earlier and more children are getting improved services faster and earlier.

A lot of parents of newly diagnosed kids don't know what they are entitled to or where to get the proper diagnosis, treatment, and services. The Autism Society directs them where to go, what to get, and what to demand when going in for an Individualized Education Program (IEP). We tell parents, "Make sure you have written in the IEP *exactly* what you want and then follow up with the Department of Education to make sure they supply that for you." The IEP is a legal document that states exactly what services will be provided, and the goals and benchmarks the teachers are to reach with that child. Update your IEP every six months. If a parent sees change or doesn't see change and wants to alter the IEP, call a special IEP team meeting, and they can make changes or get recommendations from outside sources, doctors, and therapists.

One devastating case I handled was with a 13-year-old autistic child who had slipped through the cracks. He was receiving no services whatsoever. It was a horrible situation. If he had received services since preschool, I am certain things could have turned out differently. Nevertheless, he is in the tenth grade now, and chances are that he'll end up in a group home. When I got the case, I got him every service available, but at that point it was almost too little too late because he was so old. I never gave up on him, though.

In the foster system, parents handle the task of daily care. In the foster homes I work with, I require the parents to have education or experience working with children who have disabilities. The 13-year-old I worked with had foster parents who had no clue what to do with him. When children are non-verbal, people often have the misconception that non-verbal is equal to non-thinking. Being non-verbal doesn't mean you can't communicate at all; it means you can't communicate by speaking. I tried for six months to get him into a therapeutic foster home where they knew how to treat this child, but it was impossible. He had a lot of extra needs: he was mentally retarded, in a wheelchair, and had cerebral palsy in addition to autism. As I worked with him, he began making great progress; he had even started to speak a little. However, as a result of neglect by the foster parents, he ended up having a stroke at age 14 and his condition worsened.

For six months prior to the stroke, he was saying words and responding with sign language. He could understand commands, but now he has totally regressed, all because of an untreated ear infection. The school called one afternoon and told me he was wobbling (he was walking at that point), and it seemed that his equilibrium was off. The foster parents hadn't bothered to mention that to me. Monday and Tuesday they sent him to school, and the school called me Tuesday when he was practically falling over. I immediately called the foster parents and told them, "You will take him to the emergency room and get him an MRI. Don't leave until you find out exactly what is wrong." It took them until the following Friday to take any action, and he ended up in the hospital with the damage already done.

Sadly, the stroke caused the boy to totally regress. It was very tough on me. After the stroke he could no longer walk or sit up. They put rubber mats around his room, sat him on the floor, and left him. They didn't know how to work with him, and wouldn't listen when I tried to teach them. I showed them what they needed to do with him on a daily basis, but they didn't have time for him. They complained all the time. "He's too big now. We can't do that," they'd argue. He and I used to play and wrestle. He could pin me down so I couldn't get up. When I was with him, we had fun and we communicated. I tried to teach the foster parents sign language, but they didn't want to be bothered. He's still with them, and I no longer have the case.

Regardless of the horrid circumstances, I couldn't get him removed from the home. There are just not enough foster homes out there, especially with properly trained parents. Every state is different though. In some states, foster parents have to go through a 20-week training course, but here there is no training. That's the injustice in the justice system, and the ones who suffer are the children, the ones who have no voice. That's why I am their voice, because they have nobody to speak for them. People who work in the court system don't understand about developmental disabilities. My colleagues kept asking me, "Why do you do this? Why do you work so hard?" I said, "Why wouldn't I? He's a human being. He's God's kid. Why wouldn't I?" There's no reason I could think of not to help him.

Dolly's tips

- Don't let the doctors talk over you. Make sure you feel like you are getting the advice and direction you need, and the diagnosis that will allow you to meet your child's needs.

- Keep going, don't give up, and don't stop!

CR

Jennifer, Ryan (4), and Kyle (4)

The first thing we did when we moved here was get both boys on Medicaid, and that has opened huge doors for us. There is an advocacy group here called Idaho Parents Unlimited, and I got right on the phone with them, and they directed me to all the right places. I'm so glad they exist because they've been such a help. I got a list of all the Developmental Disabilities (DD) agencies within the state and just started calling. We had a couple of interviews and found the right ones for us. We've had quite a wait for occupational therapy, but we'll be starting next week. Speech therapy we got right away. I feel like I'm on the phone all the time. It was a lot of work getting all these things set up for the boys. It was a full-time job for the first few weeks we were here because we didn't know anything. There's so much out there. I can't imagine if I had to work and do this too. I'm so thankful I'm able to stay at home; I don't know how parents who both work do it. There's so much to do. You're almost like the manager of your own business...I should be paid for this! We have a great service coordinator who is also very helpful with getting some of the therapists and finding the right doctors. We are so lucky to have great people working for us.

Presently, I'm taking a leadership course to learn to advocate more for Ryan. There are a lot of adults in my class with developmental disabilities, and they are the most amazing people. I never would have met them otherwise. There are people with cerebral palsy and people who are blind and with mild mental retardation, and they are just the most amazing people. I just wish everybody could open their eyes to that. Just because someone is different doesn't mean they are less human. I don't want anyone to think of my son that way.

I'm enrolled in the leadership class through the University of Idaho and the Idaho Council on Developmental Disabilities. It's a nine-month course, so it's quite a commitment. You go one weekend every month, and it's designed for parents, adult advocates, and adult self-advocates. The course covers the ins and outs of disabilities—everything from working with the school district to living independently. I recommend trying to find something similar to it wherever you live. The course is called Partners in Policy Making, and I am so thrilled that I was chosen for the class. I'll be going to my third session next month.

Everybody who I've met who has graduated from this course has said, "Oh, it will change your life!" At first I was doubtful, but now that I've gone to a few sessions, I can see they are right. What an eye-opener! Now I know I want to devote my life to this cause and to helping people with developmental disabilities. They shouldn't have to fight to get the things they need. If I can help one person I will.

There are things each of us can do at local, state, and national level to make a change. Through Unlocking Autism I was able to write a proclamation for the state of Idaho to proclaim April to be Autism Awareness Month, and the governor signed it, and it was passed. I never anticipated I would do anything like that in my life. Who would have believed I'd have the governor's signature hanging in my bedroom? It's the little things that you can do...and you know you *can* do it! It's in you; you might not think so, but it is.

Like I said before, this has totally changed my life. In so many ways we're so much better because all this has happened. I'm not trying to pull my own chain, not at all. I've done all this for my son, and I just try to keep things in perspective and remember all the other kids and adults I've met with autism. I'm so sick of hearing about Ryan and how he's different; I'm sick of hearing his shortcomings. There are just so many other things that are just amazing about him, and I want to celebrate those things.

Ryan smiles and this kid is worth a million bucks. When he experiences pure joy, everyone around him can feel it. He's got this million-dollar smile, and he just lights up and when he laughs it's genuine. I've never heard a kid laugh like him. When he's happy, he's amazingly happy, and when he's sad he's truly sad, but then a few minutes later he's full of joy again. He has come so far in such a short time.

In the beginning, I don't want to say I didn't have any hope, but I had no idea where we'd be in a year. Ryan couldn't even speak, but now he's starting to bloom. I've heard that the higher-functioning kids tend to reach a peak then level off for a while and then start to progress again. Growth is not necessarily continuous, it comes in spurts and plateaus, and we're definitely in a spurt right now. There's promise and potential in every child, and parents need to know that. You don't have to stick your kids in these state hospitals. There are so many things that you can do at home to help them. Keep pushing and one day you'll see something. The attention autism has gotten in the media is wonderful—with additional money and research, the future is brighter than ever before.

Jennifer's tip

- Be positive and fight for your children.

ひ

Leslie and Jared (9)

One day, my family and I were in the grocery store shopping for food, which is something my husband would typically do by himself. For some reason, we all decided to go. Jared acts differently towards each family member in the house, and I am not exactly sure why. For some reason, with the whole family he seems to act out more. Anyhow, we all decided to go to the grocery store together, as a normal family would. In my mind's eye, I can still picture Jared running down every single aisle, screaming at the top of his lungs and lying on the floor at times; he just wouldn't listen to me. He wouldn't listen to anyone for that matter. He was also determined to throw everything in the cart that he could get his hands on.

He is so big that every noise seemed to be amplified. My nine-year-old boy weighs about 101 pounds. The grocery store was so crowded, and down every aisle Jared was destroying something else and disrupting others. It got to the point where my husband had to straddle him right in the middle of the floor and do our "time out" routine in front of the whole store. Jared was screaming at the top of his lungs; I wanted to just dissolve.

A store worker came out and asked if everything was okay. Talk about frustration. I wanted to scream at him, "Does it look like everything is okay?" People were actually starting to report us at that moment. The looks on their faces were saying, "Don't they know how to handle that kid?" With all the stares, tears flowed steamily down my face. I wanted to throw up. Because of Jared's size, there was no way we could have physically carried him out of the store.

I worry about what people will think of my son. They don't hesitate to look at him with disgust. I wanted to yell, to tell people that he has something wrong with him. He wasn't just being a brat like the people assumed. On the other hand, I wanted to tackle them and say, "He has autism; why can't you just try to understand and stop judging?" I wish I could put a sticker on his forehead that says, "AUTISM." These people are adults, and I want them to understand that it is stressful for all of us and that my son can't help it. It makes me angry because I feel like I have to explain all the time. My emotions were raw, and I knew people who did not understand surrounded us.

Shortly thereafter, we turned the corner and there was a little old lady with tears streaming down her face. She had a truck in her hand and said, "I know today isn't a good day and it is hard, but I bought this for your son. Do you think it may help him to settle down?" Talk about night and day emotions. This lady went way out of her way to ask what she could do to help or what she could do to make our son happy. To her it was something simple like buying a gift for Jared. She had so much compassion that she had shed some tears for us. I can't say that the truck helped my son, but it did help me to know that some people can show some empathy and compassion. The whole scene changed within five minutes, and I was actually dumfounded with her kindness.

Eventually we managed to get Jared into the van. I was crying, Alyssa, my daughter, was crying, Jared was crying, and the only thing I could say to my husband was, "Never will we all go to the store again." It was not anyone's fault, as you can't predict what will happen. I can tell you to this day, we have never gone back to the store together again, and my husband is back to doing the grocery shopping again alone.

Since then, I have become a representative for Unlocking Autism for the state of Illinois. When parents call or email me for advice, the first thing I ask is, "How are Mom and Dad?" or "How tired is Mom?" I take some time to first encourage the parents because our needs are often overlooked in the process of getting help for our children. Collectively, we are exhausted. I usually give as much encouragement as possible and direct them to resources in their area. It is hard to get too involved with other things, because I am just still too overwhelmed with my own circumstances.

I now work with kids two hours a day at a local school helping children from low-income families who have many, many needs. I would have never wanted to work with children had it not been for Jared. I worked at a bene-fit-consulting firm for 16 years before I realized my true calling was not in the corporate world but with children. I am a very fortunate woman. I am the mother of an autistic child, and I am a better person because of it.

I will say that I used to be jealous of and angry with all of my friends who had "normal" children. I now know that I receive blessings that my friends with normal kids will never have. I am the lucky one. I can say that now…Jared is sweetly sleeping.

ɷ

Nichole and Seth (12)

Seth is a happy, silly child. He loves to memorize cartoons and even tries to tell jokes. On a typical day, Seth wakes up, goes to the bathroom, gets dressed, and makes his bed. Then he comes out of his room and asks me what he is supposed to do next. I remind him that he needs to eat breakfast.

Seth can fix his own breakfast now, but that requires me to have easy-to-prepare foods that he likes handy, which are few and far between. He won't eat cereal in milk, and he really doesn't like eggs. He will eat toast, but is afraid to pull it out of the toaster because it feels too hot. After break-fast, he will ask me what to do next. I gently remind him to brush his teeth and then get his backpack ready. During the course of all these activities, Seth is usually reciting a cartoon or joke to himself and to anyone else who will listen. If he is not telling a joke, he is usually replaying one in his head and will occasionally burst out in laughter. I then proceed to remind Seth to get his snack and put his sneakers on. The steps go on and on. The routine is exactly the same every school morning.

I definitely realized something was wrong when Seth was 18 months old. Previous to that I just considered him "colicky" and figured he would outgrow it. His sister had been born a month prior, and we started attending a playgroup in town. As I observed the group, I noticed that the other kids Seth's age were already talking quite a bit, and playing in a manner that he was not. I shared my concern with my family that something was not right, but they felt I was overreacting and told me not worry so much. I also discussed these same apprehensions with my pediatrician, but he agreed with my family's opinion. However, many of the mothers in the playgroup had experienced similar anxieties with their own children and directed me to organizations and school-related services that performed early childhood evaluations. Thanks to the playgroup, we were on our way to getting help!

In the meantime, Seth underwent a variety of evaluations through the school and the state Child Development Clinics. He had started receiving speech therapy by two years of age, along with physical and occupational therapy. All of his therapies were very limited at that time and certainly not of the intensity he needed. I also had services from our Family, Infant, and Toddler program, which at age three transitioned to the Head Start Program.

Following Seth's second birthday, I went back to college to get a nursing degree. Seth and his sister Jenna went to a wonderful home daycare, almost full-time. Seth was able to receive his therapeutic services while he was at the daycare. By the time Seth was three years old, his father and I had separated and filed for divorce. The diagnosis did not come until Seth was four and a half years old.

When Seth's diagnosis finally came, it was an interesting scenario. I was now in my last semester of nursing school. After many appointments and evaluations with Seth, the doctor diagnosed him with Asperger's Syndrome. Since I was in the medical field and knew my way around the DSM-IV, I had a problem with this diagnosis. At four and a half years old, Seth could say only two words. He clearly had a communication problem, which is one of the major differences between an Asperger's and classic autism diagnosis. To make matters worse, when the doctor gave me the diagnosis she said, "I can offer you no hope for your son's future. There is no cure."

We left the office that day, Seth's hand in mine, and stepped out into the sun. For the first time in my life, I had no clue what to do next. I was overwhelmed and totally numb. We went home that afternoon, and I sat at my kitchen table, just looking through the mound of research I had printed off, reading about autism and Asperger's. As I sat there, my phone rang and it was the Child Development Clinic. There was a doctor there who wanted to evaluate Seth; they had an opening in my area the next day and did I want to go? I told her I didn't know if we should bother, and proceeded to tell the assistant the events of the past few months. I told her everything right down to how I disagreed with the diagnosis and how I felt that, if anything, it was classic autism. I mean, heck, if he had to be diagnosed with something, let's make sure it's correct! She proceeded to tell me she really felt I should bring Seth in and then explained why. Dr. Contompasis was one of the leading authorities on autism in Vermont. He was working with Dr. Patty Prelock on a three-year program called the Rural Autism Project. I said, "We'll take the appointment." Seth was subsequently diagnosed with classic autism.

I don't think I gave myself time to react emotionally; I went right into "let's get it done" mode. What I mean by this is, I researched all the interventions, recommendations, and medications, finding out the pros and cons on everything. I was going to make sure my son got everything he needed and to the degree he needed it to give him the best possible set-up for him to achieve his best possible outcome.

Several years after Seth was diagnosed, I was working on an awareness fundraising project for Unlocking Autism. I was a state representative for Vermont. My fellow representative Cindy and I had worked with the Vermont Teddy Bear Company to create an "Aware Bear" that wore an Unlocking Autism T-shirt. Half the purchase price of the bear went to support Unlocking Autism. The biggest news station in Vermont came to interview me at my home. At one point, the reporter asked me, "What was it like and how did it feel when you first heard the diagnosis?" I had to really take a minute to think about it and put myself back to that moment. Before I could stop it, the tears were streaming down my face. All those stored-up emotions were finally coming out. Once I composed myself, I shared our story with her.

CR

Susan and Mark (10)

Delaware has a good autism program for those under the age of 21 but after 21, the services aren't as readily available. While the state legislature and community at large have been very supportive of our kids, I often worry about who will take care of Mark when we're gone. I don't want his older sister, Laura, to ever be burdened by being his complete caregiver, yet she will definitely need to be part of his life. I remember overhearing a conversation between Laura and a friend who also had a sibling with autism. They were actually discussing having to take care of their siblings when they're older. They were nine at the time!

The entire family have become autism advocates. I'm involved with three different autism groups. Our social life basically revolves around autism functions these days.

My motivation came from a desire to address the needs of children locally and nationwide. I'm hoping greater tolerance and acceptance can be found for Mark and other children like him. I also look forward to the time when people with autism will be recognized for their intrinsic worth and accepted in the community, living somewhat independently and contributing to society.

Another thing I think is important is to talk with parents and siblings about the grieving process. Similar to the stages of grief following death as defined by Kübler-Ross [see Recommended Reading section], parents of children with autism need to grieve as well. But for us, the grieving process doesn't end; each time we look at our child, we are reminded of the things we have lost. You live, you laugh, you cope and move on, but it's always there.

Susan's tips

- Talk about the grieving process—work through stages of denial, anger, bargaining, depression, and acceptance.

- Learn how to laugh and work with it.

- Take time to address the needs of siblings. Don't put pressure on them to be the perfect child, and listen to their concerns.

ભ

Terri and Nicholas (12)

Nicholas is a daddy's boy now that he is going through puberty, so they talk about books, problems, and guy stuff. They also discuss issues like homework, friends, and everyday things that need to be taken care of. Nicholas is starting to shut the door in my face because he wants more privacy. I always tell him if he does well and holds out in school, he can come home and have an autistic moment. Most of the time, Nicholas will control himself all day in school, do his homework, and then come to me and say, "I am going to be autistic now." Then he goes upstairs into his room and has his moments. He will make noises, play with cars or games, and even jump around. When it is time for dinner, he can turn it right off again and come back down and be "typical."

When Nicholas was diagnosed, I was going through the certification process to become a special education teacher. I had certain courses dealing with developmental disabilities, and we were shown movies about autism made in the 1970s where the children wore helmets and were often institutionalized. As I watched them I kept saying, "This is not my child, this is not my child." I was stunned and terrified to think that was what we had to look forward to. After about a month, I realized that the video definitely did not portray my child and was not representative of all children with autism. By that time, Nicholas had received an Asperger's Syndrome diagnosis, so I realized he was capable of much more than the movie had depicted.

Most people don't understand the word "autism." Even the most enlightened teachers will say, "No, no, not in my classroom." Nicholas's school offers occupational, physical, and speech and language therapies. In the last couple of years, some of the parents have even established a "sensory room." His school is not perfect, but it is a far step up from what other parents describe. Because I am a coordinator of special needs for the schools in the next county, and since I know the IDEA laws backward and forward, I believe they do whatever they can to accommodate Nicholas. I also serve as an advocate for parents throughout the state of Kentucky because I believe parents should not have to quote the law to get the services needed for their children.

Through my involvement in advocating for children with special needs at local and state level, I was asked to write a few articles for a magazine. We are also working on a documentary called *Nicholas' Journey*, and Nicholas is helping. The movie shows triumphs and journeys throughout his life. It's exciting to know that we can reach out and help other families who are experiencing similar things.

Nicholas loves to travel and has been to Washington twice. We were there participating in a march for autistic children to tell Congress that these children need help. We put all our money into our son, but a lot of people can't do that. We know not everyone can afford to pay for all the treatments they need, and we were lobbying to improve insurance coverage for developmental disabilities. I remember someone telling me, "Hey, your son isn't even autistic," because Nicholas was marching with us. I said, "If you can't tell he is autistic, how do you expect people to get help?"

During the march I had the opportunity to talk to one of the congress-men and voice our concerns. Ironically, it also happened to be Bring Your Daughter/Son to Work Day. Clinton was in office at the time and as the congressman and I were talking, up walks Hillary Clinton surrounded by a crowd of security officers. Not considering the ramifications, I grabbed her arm and said, "I am here for all the autistic children who can't come to work with their mothers today." I surprised myself with my boldness. The secu-rity officers came at me, and I backed off deferring, "I am sorry. I am not trying to harm her or anything." Hillary surprised me and said, "Come on into my office right now." When we arrived, she told me to call if I needed anything because she was here to help. She sat and chatted with me and even gave me her private email. It was great, and I got to tell everyone that day at a speech I gave that Hillary Clinton was on our side. I figure that if I don't speak out for those who can't, who will? I have always been an advo-cate for the underdog. This is simply a way of life.

CR

Susan, Scott, and Colton (7)

Some of the other kids don't understand Colton's behavior. Using an idea I found in an Autism Awareness Week email, I created a booklet that has some facts about autism to share with the kids in his classes. I also wrote a letter to their parents explaining the situation and included an article called "Autism: the Invisible Gift." The booklet helps the other children to under-stand autism by giving them concrete examples of how a child with autism experiences the world. For instance, I talk about what it's like to eat a peach: to you it's juicy, sweet, and wonderful, but to a person with autism it could be almost painful because of the texture or the sweetness. In the booklet I include a little picture of Colton, and the kids can color an autism aware-ness ribbon, too. Each year I go into the classroom while Colton is in resource or therapy, and I meet the kids and talk with them. In kindergar-ten, I did it at the end of the year (the suggestion came in April), but for first grade, I did it at the beginning.

During my second presentation, I gave the kids about a month to expe-rience Colton on a day-to-day basis, and then I went into the classroom and passed out the books to the children. I introduced myself by saying, "I'm here to talk about Colton. I'm his mom. Colton has autism. Do you have any questions about Colton?" They had no hesitation asking why Colton does certain things.

One of the biggest concerns is Colton's hair fetish—he loves to play with hair. In fact, he will walk up to girls, grab their hair, and put it in his face. He especially likes girls with long, silky hair. Of course they don't understand why he's messing with their hair, and it freaks them out. I told them, "He does that because he likes the texture of your hair and how it feels. He thinks your hair is very beautiful. Make sure that when Colton comes up to you he asks to touch your hair. Say, 'Colton, ask first.'" Then he's supposed to ask if he can play with her hair. If the girl says no then he stops, but if she says yes then he can go ahead and play with it. We've tried to train him that way because a few times a girl would walk by in the hallway, and he'd reach out and grab her hair. Because they are going in opposite directions, he nearly yanks it out of her head, so instead we teach him to ask. Although he's getting much better at asking first, he still forgets occasionally.

By listening to the presentation and reading the booklets, the kids begin to understand why Colton does the things he does and how he sees the world. This simple action, which takes less than an hour, changes the whole attitude in the class toward him. For me, one of the most rewarding things was hearing the teacher's description about what happened after I spoke with the children. When the kids went out to the playground for recess, the kids in his class actually taught the children from the other classes about Colton. Some of the descriptions they used and how they reworded things were very funny, but they got their point across. The teacher told me that they were now very protective of Colton and would say to the other kids, "Don't be mean to Colton because he's autistic. He just sees things differently than you do." Remember, this is first grade I'm talking about. That little effort on my part had a huge impact.

By sending the letter home to the parents, they understand that if they go to any kind of function at school or if their kid comes home and says something about Colton, they can understand what is going on and how to help their child with the situation. I know when we go out in public people look at him sideways when he's doing something weird, so it helps them understand who Colton is and why he does what he does. The note and explanation diffuse a lot of anger when their little girl goes home and says she got her hair pulled. Instead of getting Mom and Dad upset and calling the school to find out why this kid is hurting their daughter, they can help her understand that it was an accident. Some parents have gone out of their way to help. Colton's has a "girlfriend" called Katie, whose parents are wonderful individuals and they have purposely put her in Colton's classes—now as they go on to second grade, we've made sure they have the same teacher. Katie thinks he's great. She'll walk up to him and say, "Colton, do you want to play with my hair?"

School is no longer a scary situation for us. At first we were so tentative about everything—talking to the parents, creating the pamphlet and everything. Becoming more involved has been great. By addressing something before it happens, we make a potentially punitive situation educational. When I was talking about Colton to the kids, they mentioned another autistic child in his class and wondered if she had the same thing. I was able to say, "Yes, she has autism, but she probably does things differently than Colton because not all autistics act the same." It is hard for me to describe other kids, but I tried to help the children understand that she has special needs, too. Then the kids asked me, "Is Colton special?" I tell them, "All of you are special in a different way; some of you have blonde hair and some have red—having autism doesn't make Colton more special than you are. He is different, and to him it's perfectly cool to walk up to someone and pull their hair, but you understand that it's not."

Incidentally, we've chosen not to look at autism like we're victims. We take an active part in Colton's progress. We do research on the Internet, we read books, and we attend Autism Society meetings on a weekly basis. We check the message board daily to see what's going on in the autism world, and we actively keep ourselves as updated as possible. We get every autism-related newsletter from every organization out there to see if anything new is going on. Some parents we've met around here use autism as an excuse to feel sorry for themselves. They claim, "Oh my God, I can't take another day of this. Poor me." So we don't spend a lot of time with them.

Is autism frustrating? Yes, it's incredibly frustrating. Does Colton make us want to pull our hair out? Of course he does. It's still a matter of perspective, though. We tend to look at our situation with Colton and say, "Oh cool, look what he's doing today!" and we get through it together.

᎒Ꮞ

A professional's perspective: Sue Ann Kline, Director, Autism Asperger Resource Center, Kansas City, Kansas

The Autism Asperger Resource Center (AARC) is a support center that is led by professionals. We also have parents who volunteer here on a regular basis. In general, we don't specialize in a particular kind of technique; rather, we tend to try to provide unbiased recommendations and suggest interventions based on each individual child's needs. Many centers are specific to ABA, dietary needs, or something else. There aren't a whole lot of places where parents can go and do their own research about what might be out there, other than the Internet. We are unique in that way.

Although the center is located in a hospital, we are not officially affiliated with the hospital. We're a non-profit organization. However, when a child receives a diagnosis at the hospital, a staff member can walk him upstairs to where we are located for that "What's next?" step. We find assistance during the period following diagnosis is crucial for parents and children. Many parents are going through such stress and grieving it's difficult to focus on finding information on their own.

Lots of parents say things like, "If my child had a cold I'd know what to do, but my child has autism, and I have no clue what to do." Often the places that do want to help charge enormous sums of money, but there are only a few information and support-based resource centers. That is the thing that makes us different. We work with many of the hospitals in the area, and we are on their referral lists—so if a child has been diagnosed and the parents contact us we can automatically tell them some things to do. We believe that this type of service is necessary in all states, and we are advocating with the government for that because there is just not enough help available for parents.

We completed some research for senators and representatives, and found out that while there are many support groups—for example, the Autism Society of America—they do not have chapters in all 50 states. For instance, here in Kansas we have only two chapters serving the entire state. Even in a state as large as California there are only 15 chapters and most of those are parent led. Parent resource groups provide an invaluable service, but on the other hand, it can be beneficial to have someone who's not personally affected to be able to come in and say, "Here's what the research says about this particular technique, and here are the names of three people who can help. Here's what you can do." We find that parents are not always able to do that. They can say, "This is what happened for my child," but as you know, every child is different. That's another way we're different.

At our center, we have a process called "intake" where parents can come in and have a free visit with a consultant who will sit down with the family, listen to their story, write a few notes about what the child needs, and from that we'll develop a list of recommendations and resources for them. When we began offering the service we thought only newly diagnosed families would want to do it, but we've found that parents at nearly every step of the way want to come back and review information. For example, during the transition to high school, a child's needs change, or when they transition to the world of work they may have completely different needs. Many families come back every year and go through the process again. They want to talk. They want to tell their story, and they want to discuss what's changed in their child's life, and we help them develop a new list of resources and address their concerns.

For the past nine years, the center has also sponsored a summer camp. Camp Determination is an overnight camp for children aged 8 through 18 who have autism or Asperger's Syndrome. We offer a 1:1 camper to staff ratio. In order to find qualified staff, we work with the local colleges and bring in psychology, speech, language pathology, special education, and occupational therapy students to be our camp counselors. We get an incredibly professional, energetic, and highly talented group of young people to come in, and they do it completely free. They spend the whole week with the kids—and in return get training, experience, and meet other people in the field. Everybody wins! We could not continue to do camp without the number of volunteers. Every year it is an incredible experience for everyone involved.

Sue Ann's tip

- Get connected to a resource center that can give you information and support. Being part of the autism community makes a huge difference. You instantly feel like part of a family. This community is very strong, and once people get involved, they will find incredible support, information, and networking. It is so much harder to do it on your own. Get connected!

To contact Sue Anne for further information, go to www.autismasperger.org.

SOMETHING TO TALK ABOUT

1. I'm getting to the point where I finally feel like I've got things under control. How can I help other parents?

2. What are the best groups to become involved with locally/within the state/nationwide to become active in raising awareness about autism, education, politically, and for personal support?

3. What are some ideas for dealing with people in public places who do not understand why my autistic child is acting this way?

4. How should I go about becoming involved with policy making/improving the laws regarding children with developmental disabilities?

5. What autism awareness programs could I help bring to my area?

REFLECTION ACTIVITY

Get involved in an autism awareness project, either online or locally. Be sure to decide on a specific amount of time you are willing to contribute on a weekly basis and then do it! You'll be amazed how great you feel helping others.

8.

Is There Anybody Out There?
How Our Faith has
Helped Us Through

Barbie and John Matthew (10)

For the summer, we enrolled John Matthew in Vacation Bible School (VBS) through a church in town. My neighbor belongs to the church and encouraged me to let him attend, promising to keep an eye on him. I was hesitant because John Matthew has always attended a very small *Little House on the Prairie*-type school (a total of 60 kids in grades K to 8), and I wondered if the number of children would be overwhelming.

As luck would have it, at this VBS they start and end at the same place every day. On the first morning, looking in I could see the sanctuary contained pew after pew of noisy, excited kids. I literally had to drag John Matthew through the chapel doors. He was holding my hand tight and trembling a bit but not saying anything, and I knew he was stressed. My neighbor had informed the leader for his age group a little about John Matthew, so she was prepared. She came right up to him and said, "John Matthew come sit by me," and took care of him. I left feeling incredibly nervous, wondering if he'd survive the day.

When I went back to pick John Matthew up three hours later, he was with his class in the front pew surrounded by a couple hundred other kids. Some teenage girls were up on the stage singing and doing hand motions, and music was blaring. All the kids were standing up, and I could barely see him over their heads. John Matthew was doing everything right along with the rest of the group. He was singing and clapping, and had the biggest smile on his face. He turned around and noticed me standing there. John Matthew and I have a secret sign for "I love you" (in sign language). He held his little hand up and did the sign and just kept going. He went back every day that week without any incidents. He loved it!

CR

Jennifer, Colin (4), and Cameron (4)

I pray all the time for God to help me to help Colin and Cameron. I pray for strength. I pray that God will show me what needs to be done, and when I do that, things go my way. I have faith that I was given these children for a reason, and because they were given to me, I will be given the tools to handle it. I have faith—you either have it or you don't. I had it before they were diagnosed and dealing with autism has simply made it stronger.

Now that I have the boys, I don't go to church every week. I have faith that my children are being guided and protected. My mantra is, "God, please help me get through this." I've had some hard times, but there is no doubt in my mind that someone is watching out for me.

CR

Sophie and Ben (10)

Honestly, if it wasn't for our faith and my membership in the Church of Jesus Christ of Latter-Day Saints, I would have exploded, "Forget it, that's it!" more than once. My faith teaches me to think that there's a purpose for Ben being like this and for us to help him. The purpose for me is that our Heavenly Father sent him to us so that we could learn something and become different and better. That's my take on it, at least.

For instance, I teach English as a Second Language. My students tell me I am so patient. I think, "Me, patient?" Then I look back at myself and, compared with how I was before all these issues with Ben began, I realize I am patient. I really have come a long way. Not to toot my own horn or anything, it's just amazing how I really have changed in a positive way. I say to them, "Helping you learn English is nothing. Try potty training a six-year-old!" but they don't understand. In their eyes I'm still the most patient person they know.

When things get out of control I can pray and read the scriptures, and gain some sort of peace amidst the craziness. When my faith is not up to par, I struggle and question God, "Why does this have to happen to me? Why does this have to be so hard?" Other times I am stronger, and I recognize how lucky I am to have the gospel to bring me perspective. Other people are stuck in this kind of thinking all the time. Without a higher power to turn to, they probably feel like there is no hope.

An acquaintance, whose child was in Ben's class, had a philosophy that was completely different than mine. Everything she said about her child was negative. Instead of enjoying when we were together, her constant negativity was dragging me down. She viewed autism with so much bitterness I had to stop having any contact with her. I felt like I was letting her down, but it was a matter of survival for me. Personally, I have to stay focused on the fact that I am supposed to learn something from everything we are going through and better myself through this experience.

When I am actively engaged in improving things for Ben, I am less likely to become negative and get stuck in a "Why me?" mentality. Honestly, you know that everything has been worth it when you are having a bad day and your once non-verbal child comes up to you and asks, "What's wrong, mom?" There is nothing in the world that can compare to that!

Sophie's tip

- Keep going. Don't give up!

CR

Karen and Dylan (7)

I remember one day I was really upset over something Dylan did. I was at one of my lowest points, and I confided to my husband, "I don't know what I did to make God so angry with me, but I'm sorry." My husband said, "This is not a punishment, and God is not punishing you." I said, "Then what is he trying to teach me?" and he said, "He already has."

"What could I possibly learn from this?" I asked.

His answer was a revelation to me, as he said, "Compassion and patience. You never had either one of those before Dylan came along." I just stared at him; his insight left me speechless.

Dylan has taught me things I never knew I needed to learn. Before he came along, I was a perfectionist who expected the rest of the world to be perfect. I'd never been dealt any hardships. I don't feel sorry for myself. Autism is not about being punished or doing the wrong thing. This is the card you were dealt, and you have to play your hand. That's not to say I don't have days when I say, "I don't want to do this any more, I quit!" Then I pick myself up and say, "Karen, you don't have a choice." People say stuff like, "I don't know how you do it!" to me and I feel like responding, "Oh, I have a choice?" No kids come with a money-back guarantee. I can't trade him in, and wouldn't want to for that matter. I made my choice when he was conceived.

CR

Leslie and Jared (9)

What makes our journey all worth it is Jared's unconditional love and his sweet, sweet face. God gave me a "sixth sense" to know something was wrong with Jared at a very early age, even when everyone said there was nothing wrong with him. God gave me grace to do the right things at the right time, and the grace not to fall on my face. I can't imagine going one day without knowing that God's grace is sufficient for me. I have claimed that and believe it with every fiber of my soul. God has blessed me through my son in ways I could have never imagined. I also lean on my counselor as well as other parents in my support systems. Jared is doing well in school, but he needs help with his social skills. We will have him in camp for autistic children this summer, thanks to a scholarship received from the special education district.

I will say God has given me a dose of patience that I would have never expected. In my spare time, I volunteer to assist children from low-income families. I counsel, listen, and pray with these children, and God gives me strength in the battleground.

CR

Theresa and Josiah (7)

At our house, Sundays are church days. Josiah regularly attends Sunday school with me as his aide. He will begin asking to go to church as soon as he gets up on Sunday and does not let up until we arrive there. He loves the music and the puppets. When Josiah was two, we left a church we had attended for nine years because they asked us not to bring Josiah as he was disruptive. We now attend a church that has welcomed Josiah despite his behavior, and the church members have loved us through the most difficult times.

Many people who we once thought were friends stopped calling and inviting us over due to Josiah's unpredictable behavior. They have been replaced over time with new friends who love us unconditionally. I also was forced to alter my expectations in terms of relationships with family members as some relatives also chose not to allow Josiah into their homes. Through our challenges with Josiah, I have developed the ability to love others in spite of their faults. Other changes that have occurred include abandoning my former career ambitions in order to be a full-time mother. Surprisingly, I found that I have not lost anything in doing so. I have been blessed in so many ways by raising all of our boys.

My greatest fears are that someday Josiah's behaviors will become so aggressive that he will need to be placed in a residential care facility or perhaps even a correctional facility. I cling to my faith in Jesus as I pray that Josiah will be known as a man of gentleness and kindness. When you have a child kicking, biting, hitting, throwing things, and punching holes in walls, my dream becomes harder to envision. I pray that he will gain the social skills to be able to have friends, become a productive part of society, live independently, and share his life experiences with others.

My greatest source of strength and support is my relationship with Jesus. Without my faith, I could not face this journey. There is so much peace in knowing that God has a plan and purpose for my life. He holds me in His hands and is there to lift me up when I think I cannot go on.

Fortunately I also have a great network of support. My sister Marie, who also has a special needs child, has been a constant source of strength and encouragement. My friends from East Auburn Baptist Church have walked with me all the way, holding me up in prayer and helping me to find hope and peace. They have fed my spirit so that I have the strength to keep walking. The staff at Margaret Murphy Center for Children (MMCC) and other specialists have helped me grow in my understanding of Josiah and to find resources to help us as a family. They have loved Josiah and supported me no matter how awful Josiah's behavior has been at times.

I have learned to find joy in almost any situation, although it is a struggle to see the level of anxiety that Josiah experiences each day, including the tantrums, aggression, and destruction. I am overjoyed that he can communicate, show emotions, read, and connect with others. I am thankful that Josiah is verbal, can tell jokes, and is able to live with us. Josiah is the most grateful and appreciative child I have ever met. It takes so little to make him happy. I have learned more about life and myself through this journey than I could ever hope to teach him. He truly is a gift from God. By us having Josiah, I learned to trust myself and to not allow myself to be swayed by every judgment, criticism, and piece of advice that was handed to me.

As I said before, I could not face this every day without faith in Christ Jesus. He has given me eyes to see the blessing Josiah is. He has given me words of wisdom when I didn't know which way to turn. He has strengthened my body and mind to fight for my son. He has met every need we have had, and has helped us to learn the difference between a want and a need. He has filled me with hope for the future. He has taught me the blessing of unconditional love, not only for myself but also for my son. In every place that I am weak, He has been my strength. When I have despaired, He has been the lifter of my head. He has dried my tears. Time and time again, He has been the answer when I could not find my way.

CR

Anne and Alex (11)

Alex was our miracle baby, our only child. We had many miscarriages both before and after he was born. He was breech, so he was born by C-section and delivered two weeks early. He surprised everyone by coming earlier than the planned date. After he was born, he developed an infection and was given antibiotics. Three days later, he still wasn't eating right. The doctor, who is also a good family friend, said, "We're going to have to run some tests," and found the infection so Alex stayed in the hospital a little longer than I did.

When I look back, I was the typical first-time mom and wrote everything down. From Alex's first word to his first poop in the potty, everything is there. At age one, he would say a few words, his favorite being "no." All of a sudden, he stopped saying even that. He stopped waving. People kept telling me that for some kids it just takes longer for them to talk. Allen, my husband, and I were never big talkers, so we assumed maybe we weren't talking enough. We'd come up with things to do with him that would give us more opportunities to prompt him to talk or give some feedback, but he never really did. Finally, when I took him in for a check-up close to his second birthday, our family physician recommended we check into things a little more, and thinking it might be hearing loss, he sent us to a specialist. We went and did the test, and all the results indicated that his hearing was normal. However, they started running some other tests, and that is when they came up with the diagnosis of autism.

My dad was a minister, and my parents were good at teaching us that not everything in life is going to be the way you want it to be. For some reason or another, things in life happen, and you have to put the best construction possible on the situation you are given. When Alex was first diagnosed with autism I was bitter. I was angry with God, thinking, "We have one child, and this is what you are going to do to me?" That attitude made things tough. Going to church helped, and we tried to rely on what we'd been taught growing up because both my husband and I had pretty strong faith. We realized that certain people within our church would support us and help us through. By talking with us, praying with us, and reassuring us, they made a big impact.

The experts tell us that at this point in our marriage, since we have a child with a particular diagnosis, we should be divorced by now. Sometimes Allen and I look at each other and ask, "How *do* we make it through on a daily basis?" Between work and the exhaustion level at home there is virtually no time left for the two of us. I can totally understand how a couple without any support structure wouldn't make it through. Without our faith I don't know if we would still be together. The commitment we made to God and to each other to stay together and do what is most important for our child has helped us make it through the tough times. The child is crucial.

There have definitely been some very special people in the world that God put into our lives to help us cope as a family with autism. Unfortunately, there are other people in our church who don't quite understand what's wrong with Alex. Many of them are still from that generation of thinking, "If you don't understand something don't make it your problem." I taught Sunday school from the time I was 14 until I turned 40. When the church needed another Sunday school teacher this past year, the gal who was running the program told us that one of us needed to teach Alex or we needed to find a teacher for his class on our own. Ouch! I don't think she meant to be hurtful; I think in this case she is just ignorant and doesn't realize how much families with children who have disabilities rely on the people they go to church with to be a source of support.

Conditions like that can challenge your faith, but I'm a staunch believer that all things are done for a reason, and if this is God's plan, I need to muddle through the bad days. At some point and time He's going to reveal to me why He made certain decisions. Sometimes when I deal with parents in the classroom where I teach I wonder why certain parents have children when they want nothing to do with them. I pray, "Thank you God for giving Alex to me," because I sure wouldn't want them to have him. They'd be the type of parents to put him in an institution and never see him again. I don't think any child deserves that.

Every child has something special about him that makes him who he is. No matter what our level of ability, we all contribute something unique to the world. There have been many traumatic things that have occurred in my life, and after Alex was diagnosed on top of everything else, at one point I asked God, "What are you trying to do to me?" Now I've had time to sit back and reflect on our situation, and I know other people have it a lot worse than I do. I try to count my blessings. I asked for a beautiful child, and God gave me a beautiful child. I know sometimes I need to be less judgmental and more accepting of what happens in my life and who God has placed in it to help me. God has given us wonderful people who have made a huge difference in our lives and in Alex's life, and for that I am very thankful.

☙

A professional's perspective: Pastor Matthew Hummel, St. Steven's Lutheran Church, Wilmington, Delaware

My older brother Darrell has autism, so throughout my childhood I was keenly aware of what was done on his behalf. During my training in the seminary, I kept thinking there ought to be more for children like him. In my master's program one of the assignments was called "Ministry in Context" and involved planning and implementing a program from beginning to end. With an extensive project on the horizon, addressing the needs of people with developmental disabilities seemed a logical choice, and the SonRise service was born.

One Sunday per month our church holds a special worship service for people with autism and related disabilities and their family members. The half-hour service includes singing, prayer, litany, and a brief spiritual message. People from all denominations are invited to attend. An important aspect of the service is that no one pays attention to vocalizations or repetitive behaviors. We expect and encourage people to get up and walk around if necessary and we make accommodations accordingly. For instance, if there is a lot of noise, I talk a little louder or if someone comes up behind me while I am preaching, I may stop talking for a minute to help him back to his seat. Everyone is in the same boat. We also make sure those who attend know they are welcome at any service and that we consider them a vital part of the congregation.

For those of you who are attending a typical congregation, there are several things I recommend in order to alleviate stress and increase the likelihood of having a positive experience while at church. First and foremost, schedule a meeting with the ecclesiastic leader to discuss your child's needs and abilities. Since you have an Individualized Education Program (IEP) with specific goals, share that as well. You may even want to encourage the leader to contact the school and find out what they think would work in a church setting. Also, inform him of any medications that might impact your child's performance and participation. By doing this, the pastor knows what to expect and can meet your child's needs and address any concerns that arise within the congregation.

As far as other members are concerned, there will be times when they say things that are insensitive, regardless of how much you prepare. From personal experience, I believe the majority of questions are motivated by heartfelt concern, no matter how ineptly they may be worded. When you make it past the desire to say something in retaliation, you can often go on to have a mutually beneficial and meaningful exchange. Unfortunately, unless the person has had experience with autism specifically, they usually have no idea how offensive they are being.

According to Martin Luther, "he who comprehends the visible and manifest things of God seen through suffering and the cross" knows the nature of God. Remember God is with you, especially in the midst of a disability. Each of us is created in the image of God, which applies as fully to the kid who rocks herself and vocalizes through mass as it does to you or me. By understanding these premises, you can understand the place of your autistic child within any congregation.

SOMETHING TO TALK ABOUT

1. How has your relationship with God or a higher power changed since your child was diagnosed?

2. What has your experience attending worship services/relating to clergy been like since the diagnosis?

3. Many parents allude to the fact that God had something for them to learn from this experience. What have you learned? How has having a child with autism made you a better person?

4. Many people compare receiving a diagnosis and the ensuing emotions to those that occur following the death/loss of a child (i.e. grief, denial, anger, acceptance). How does faith play a role in the grieving process?

REFLECTION ACTIVITY

- Read the scriptures of your faith from beginning to end. Set a goal for completion within the next year. If you do not subscribe to a particular faith, read a book or attend a meeting to promote spiritual awareness.

- Using index cards or a poster board, keep a record in a visible place of things you are grateful for. Review daily—add at least one new item a day.

9.

Autism is No Laughing Matter: Finding Humor in Our Daily Lives

Angelique and Matthew (6)

I remember when I was trying to potty train Matthew. He was almost three, and he had a bowel movement on the bathroom floor instead of the toilet. When he came out of the restroom, he was holding his poop, and I thought it was a piece of chocolate that he wanted to show to me. Then I realized what it was, and I freaked. I didn't know what to do, and I smacked his wrist trying to knock it out of his hand. Instead, it went right up and hit the ceiling. He was devastated!

Another time, Matthew was searching through his baby brother Caleb's drawer and found the diaper rash ointment. Obviously he thought it felt good on his skin because he proceeded to take off all his clothes and smear the whole tube of cream over his entire body, face, and hair. He looked like a ghost. When I saw him, I couldn't help but laugh. The stuff was so oily it wouldn't wash out of his hair, so I ended up shaving his head.

CR

Jaimee and Matthew (4)

Matthew can be very amusing and stubborn at the same time. One thing I think is funny about having kids with autism is that it is great exercise for the brain. Talk about the world's longest brainteaser! I remember one time Matthew was asking me to help him spell what I thought was "Eddie elephant" (a character from a TV show), but every time I spelled Eddie, he would scream and throw a huge fit. This went on for an hour, and eventually he was so wound up I had to call my hubby home from work to help me settle him down. This little activity went on for the next few weeks as I tried to figure out what I was doing wrong. Then one day, I overheard him playing a computer game about animals and he started saying, "Eddie elephant." Finally, it all clicked. He was talking about an Indian elephant! After three weeks of tantrums, it was a relief to figure that one out.

ɔʀ

Janis and Jared (6)

I call Jared my "sunny son" because he was born on June 22, the day after the summer solstice, with 23 hours of sun in Alaska. He definitely shines warmth into our lives. There is never a dull moment. His diffluent speech and off-the-wall sayings such as, "Mickey likes to eat underwear," and "You're a chicken boy," often add a smile to our days. He is always on the go: playing, loving, teasing, and twirling.

At six years old, Jared is starting to show a sense of humor. Lately he's even been attempting to tell jokes. He realizes now that things are funny. Today, because he was so dehydrated from being sick all weekend, we had to take a urine sample. After he was done, I put it on the back of the toilet, washed my hands, and went to call the doctor who wanted a report on what Jared had done. The next thing I know, Jared comes up to me with the cup of urine with the lid on it. He smiled a huge smile and said, "Look, Mom, I made it just for you!"

ɔʀ

Julie and Jake (7)

We had just relocated to Ohio from Seattle and moved into an established neighborhood where everyone else on the block had lived for some time. It was very difficult to go out and meet people since I had to be locked up in the house for the most part while Jake was awake. I couldn't possibly have a decent conversation with someone next door with an autistic child by my side. What kind of substantial information could I possibly cram in to two minutes before Jake started darting wherever his little heart desires? Therefore, my only confidant in the area was my homeopathic doctor.

At one appointment, I was dumping my troubles on the doctor and telling him how my new neighbors probably thought we were crazy. Every time I put Jake in the car, he would let out a blood-curdling scream at the top of his lungs and start kicking me. I figured from the odd stares they gave me they would call Children Services soon and report that I was a child beater. When I was telling him this, he looked at me for a second and he started cracking up laughing! Then I joined him! We laughed until we cried and couldn't stop. I remember that day because it felt so good to laugh like that again.

We decided to take Jake and his sister Stephanie to the zoo, and Jake ended up biting another child while we were there. The child's parent told me that he "needed to be locked up in a cage, not those animals!" I got teary eyed for a moment, then I started to laugh. I told her that he was updated on all of his shots and that was the truth! Nevertheless, laughter is always good medicine. And yes, there are classic stories to tell your children when they get older about what they were like at a certain age, autistic or not!

ᙦ

Kim and Caitlynn (6)

When Caitlynn was about four and a half years old, we were at my place of employment, which was Sears Portrait Studio. I was talking to my boss when Caitie went into the camera room to play with the props on display for picture taking. She was in there happily playing for about 15 minutes and then came running out of the camera room buck-naked. She tried to run from me, but I grabbed her and threw her back into her clothes.

She then went back in to the camera room and started playing well again, although you would have thought I would have learned my lesson. I sat down to nurse my new baby daughter and the next thing I know, Caitie goes flying out of the camera room buck-naked again and right past me still nursing the baby. I stand up, hand the baby to my boss, put myself back together, and tear off after her. She was so fast that by the time I got to her, she was downstairs in linens. I borrowed a towel, wrapped her up and once again took her back and got her dressed. We left shortly after that as I had had about as much excitement as I could take that day. I must say that she sure had fun!

ᙦ

Karen and Dylan (7)

My husband and I try to find some humor in autism. We laugh about certain things Dylan does. I don't mean laugh as in not take it seriously, we just try to find the humor in the situation. For example, Dylan's nickname is

"Hooch" because when he was little he was so out of control he was like that dog from the Tom Hanks film *Turner and Hooch*. He would get in the pantry and dump everything out. There would be flour all over the floor. He was a mess! One day we were watching that movie and my older son Logan said, "Well, I'll be, Dylan acts just like that dog!" and the name stuck. Now he's Hooch. People say, "How can you call your son that?" and my reply is, "Well, you know, it just stuck."

I was in this department store, and I saw a T-shirt that said, "Just be happy I'm not your kid!" I bought it, and I put Dylan in it all the time when we go out in public. Instead of getting upset when people stare at him, I can laugh about it because I am sure that is what they are thinking. With the way he acts they are probably saying, "Good God, I'm glad he's not mine!" So we try to find some humor in a difficult situation.

Another interesting thing about Dylan is that he is very sensitive to pressure. I'm convinced he is a human barometer. He is the best meteorologist in the state of Arkansas. He even outdoes our local weatherman. I told my husband one night, "I don't know what's going on with the weather but you better batten down the hatches because it's going to get ugly." We had a tornado! Dylan doesn't tell me with words; it's his behavior. When the weather turns ugly, in watching him you'd think he has an electric current going through his system—all the hairs on his body stand up and he becomes very stiff and robotic, but at the same time he can't sit still. He has to remain in constant motion and, in a very stiff manner, he starts bouncing off the walls. If we had a chandelier, he'd probably swing from it.

His behavior gets so weird, it's hard to explain, but his teachers have picked up on it, too. They've learned to rely on Dylan to know whether it's going to rain or not. He was acting a little odd earlier today, so I told my husband, "We might actually get some rain like the people on the news are saying. Dylan's acting very agitated today." People call me on the phone to plan their weekend, "How's Dylan acting—you think it's going to rain?" For the longest time, I've wanted to email the weatherman and tell him my son is in tune with the weather; he knows when the barometer's dropping.

We love Dylan unconditionally. He is who he is, but in a lot of ways the autism is his personality. One minute I want to scream, and the next minute he's making me laugh. It's such a rollercoaster of emotions with him, so we choose to find humor and laugh about it, accept it and move on. I never feel sorry for myself, and I don't want anybody feeling sorry for me or pitying me because of Dylan. He's the joy of our lives.

CR

Nancy and Christina (6)

I can tell so many stories about Chrissy, but will try to limit myself to only a couple. We went to the Social Security office because I received a notice that Chrissy was overpaid on her SSI. When we got there, the gentlemen said, "Christina owes $1500." Then Chrissy pipes up, "I don't have any money!" Standing up on her tiptoes, she said, "Look at me, I can't! You see I am just a little kid, and I don't work." Then, jutting her chin out, she says, "Pop-pop will pay you, he has a job." The gentleman behind the desk was trying so hard not to laugh.

Chrissy is a very loving child and accepts everyone, usually. When someone is mean to her or she thinks they are, she will yell, "You're fired!"

CR

Nicole and Cole (5)

My son Cole has always been sensitive to certain noises, such as trains, blow dryers, and loud music. We've all been in those public restrooms with the toilets that flush by themselves. The first time Cole encountered one of them he was about three years old. Shocked and bewildered, he came out of the stall with his pants down, hands over his ears, looking very concerned. I reassured him that everything was okay, but I made sure from that day on, that whenever we went into a public restroom with automatically flushing toilets, I held my hand over the motion sensor until Cole was finished and out of the stall.

One sunny July afternoon, the kids and I went to the playground near our house. It was beautiful outside, and the park resembled an elementary school at recess. There had to have been at least 60 people there. Cole decided he was going to go to the bathroom by himself, so he walked across the park towards the restrooms. He stopped just outside the door and screamed at the top of his lungs, "Mommy! Do these toilets flush by themselves?" As just about every adult and half the kids turned toward me with bewildered looks on their faces, I yelled back, "No Cole, they don't flush by themselves, it's okay."

I'm sure the other parents thought Cole's question was odd, but I appreciated the progress he had made since that first encounter with the infamous self-flushing toilet.

CR

Richard and Sarah (12)

We regularly purchase Happy Meals for the free toys, because Sarah won't eat the food. As we all know, McDonald's advertises particular Happy Meal toys to attract the children, but some toys are practically impossible to get. One time, Sarah was having a tough time in school and her birthday was coming up. We promised her that if she did well in school, we were going to get her a Cinderella play set for her birthday from the Disney Store (we've learned a lot about the power of positive reinforcement!). Within the play set were three mice; they were the characters that Sarah really wanted. For weeks she kept repeating the mantra, "Three mice, three mice." Unfortunately, I learned the coveted gift was on back order and would not be available until well after Sarah's birthday. A promise is a promise, right? What a dilemma!

Around that same time, McDonald's was celebrating 100 years of Disney and within the collection of Happy Meal toys were Cinderella's three mice friends. These mice were the only things Sarah talked about from that point on. Unbelievably, there were 100 different Disney toys in the promotion, and they were available at McDonald's for 30 days only. To make matters worse, the characters were packaged in a solid white wrapper so you could not pick your toy. I found myself thinking, "How can anyone possibly get 100 toys in 30 days? You'd have to eat there for breakfast, lunch, and supper." I figured the only thing I was going to get eating at McDonald's for 30 days in a row was 30 extra pounds! The only thing I really wanted were the three mice for my beloved daughter.

True to my word, I went to every single McDonald's in my area several times a day for the next month and still did not get all three mice. I finally contacted McDonald's directly in an attempt to get one of the mice. No luck! We have been scouring yard sales and flea markets since that time and, to this day, we have still not found the whole set. I compare my quest for the illusive Happy Meal toys to the process of obtaining the services for our children. We know that they are out there, but somehow still out of reach.

❧

Terri and Nicholas (12)

Nicholas just loves to travel and does well at it. One time over the summer, a girlfriend and I took Nicholas on a driving road trip for weeks around the world. As we were driving, a police officer pulled us over due to something silly such as our plates were covered and he was unable to see the sticker. The policeman walked up to the window, knocked on it, then proceeded to ask my friend her for her registration and driver's license. Nicholas, not bashful at all and very forthright, started yelling at the officer, "Don't take her to jail or arrest her!" He adamantly insisted the officer should not arrest her, and yelled at him to go away. My friend was trying to hold back laughter, while explaining to the officer at the same time that Nicholas is autistic.

I kept telling Nicholas that it was okay and he wouldn't take her to jail, but he kept on insisting to the officer that he was being "bad" by harassing my friend. We eventually got things settled and drove away, giggling the whole time.

The first time I knew Nicholas understood revenge was when he got in trouble and had a four-minute time out. The next day, my husband called me at Nicholas's school where he was volunteering and said, "I was standing here in the bathroom with Nicholas when he just turned around and peed in the garbage can. What do I do?" I told him to ask Nicholas why he did it. Joe asked him, and he said, "To get back." That was the first time I realized he really knew what the concept of getting even was.

℞

Theresa and Josiah (7)

Josiah went through a phase where he loved to make "cakes." He would take items from the pantry and mix them together. One day, he wanted to make a cake and asked for flour. I looked at him and told him we didn't have any more flour because he had used it all. He walked over to one of my plants, hauled it out of the pot, and said, "Flower, we have flower." The look on his face was so innocent and sincere.

℞

Maria and Shea (10)

Now that my Shea is ten, I can use delayed gratification to motivate her behavior. For instance, this week she is going to summer camp, and I said, "If you have a great week at camp, then we can go to the Disney Store and get the *Mousercise* video you want." When we started out she only had to do one thing to get the reinforcer she wanted; now we're up to a whole week.

Lately, her behavior has been challenging in a different way; she's gotten much bolder with adolescence approaching. She says things like, "I'm not Shea, I'm Faye!" when she knows she's misbehaving. I'll say, "Shea, you can't do that," and she'll say, "I'm not Shea, I'm Faye...*I am not my name!"* My husband just laughed when I told him and said, "That's very philosophical. She understands that if she is not her name she doesn't have to stop being bad."

On a similar note, the other day Shea said, "I am not my name, I'm Tommy!" So I remind her that she is a girl, but she still insists she is a boy. She doesn't want to be a girl because all the other kids in her class are boys. Recently, she had to start wearing a sports bra. Now she says, "I don't want to wear a bra; I don't want to be a girl." She calls her breasts nu-nus. I told Shea when you get nu-nus, you have to wear a bra. Then she said, "I don't want to wear a bra. I want to be a Toys 'R' Us kid! Toys 'R' Us kids don't wear bras." We passed the sports bra display at Wal-Mart, and she screamed, "No bra. *No bra!"*

I can already tell puberty is going to be fun. All my friends have boys and they laugh, "Ha ha, you have to deal with a period." And I joke back and say, "Ha ha, you have to deal with him touching himself. If she has her period, nobody's going to know she's having her period, but when he's standing over there touching himself in the middle of church choir, you're going to be more embarrassed than me!"

Some of the craziest people I've met are parents of children with autism. I think maybe it's because they've had to deal with all this. Then again, maybe they are already crazy and that's why their kids are like this. I wonder sometimes—maybe genetics are involved in this one!

SOMETHING TO TALK ABOUT

1.   How can having a sense of humor make living with a child with autism easier?

2.   What is the funniest thing that has happened in regard to your child with autism?

3.   What can you do to get past the why me/crisis mode and actually start enjoying life again?

4.   Talk about the last time you really laughed or had a great time.

REFLECTION ACTIVITY

With a friend or spouse check out and watch a copy of the funniest movie you can think of. Laugh until it hurts!

Epilogue

On April 15, 2006 I found myself in the emergency room of East Tennessee Children's Hospital with my four-and-a-half-month-old daughter, Adria. She had been having seizures for the past month and that morning she'd had five of them before 8:00 in the morning. After spending six hours in the emergency room she was officially admitted as a patient. After meeting with numerous doctors who administered a myriad of tests including an MRI I remained positive.

The next day my husband, Jared, and I spent over an hour with the neurologist who explained the diagnosis—a rare genetic disorder known as tuberous sclerosis. As she described the possible consequences of the tumors growing in my little girl's brain, which may include developmental delays, intellectual delays, and autism-like behaviors, I was amazed at the calm I felt. It was if I had been there before and I knew I could handle it. Later I realized I had, in fact, lived this situation over and over in my mind as I read and reviewed the stories for this book—your stories! I knew I wasn't alone. I was standing on the shoulders of giants.

Donna Satterlee Ross

Appendix A

Interview Questions

1. (History) What is your name? What is your child's name? Age? How many siblings? Birth order of affected child?

2. How would you describe your child? Describe a typical day.

3. When did you realize something was wrong?

4. What did you do when you realized something was wrong?

5. How long did it take from when you first realized something was wrong until diagnosis? Treatment?

6. Where/how did you receive the diagnosis autism/Asperger's/PDD?

7. What was your reaction?

8. What books did you find most helpful? Least helpful?

9. How has your life changed?

10. How has your family's life changed?

11. How has your marriage changed?

12. What are your fears? Hopes? Dreams?

13. What is the hardest part of having a child diagnosed with autism?

14. What is the best part?

15. If you had to do it over, what would you do differently?

16. What about your relationships with friends and parents, and how have they changed?

17. Where do you go for support? Who provides the most support?

18. How has your faith helped you cope with the diagnosis?

19. How do you feel about your child's current level of functioning?

20. Describe a vivid memory or experience with your child that other parents of children with autism could relate to.

21. What question did you expect me to ask that I didn't ask?

Appendix B

Weekly Relationship Inventory

1. Review any calendar issues: appointments, commitments, scheduled date night.

2. Set personal and couple goals for the upcoming week.

3. Discuss openly and honestly your feelings toward one another.

   - Allow your spouse/partner to fully express his or her opinions. Do not interrupt.

   - Make sure you understand your spouse/partner's point before expressing your own.

   - Use a kind voice, but be candid and honest in your language.

   - Listen without criticizing.

   Remember:

   - Treat your spouse/partner as you would like to be treated.

   - Arrive upon decisions together whenever possible; don't issue demands and orders.

   - Make sure both partners feel valued and that they are making a contribution to the family.

Appendix C

Guidelines for Creating
a Support Group

Considerations

- For whom is the group designed?

- What will be the main goal of the group?

- Where and when will the group be held? How long will it last?

- What follow-up procedures will you use to ensure that anyone who attends will feel welcome?

Recruitment

Personal contact tends to be the best way to recruit potential members. However, flyers, newspaper advertisements, and the Internet can also be successful ways to reach your community.

By establishing contacts with clinicians, teachers, professors, doctors, ministers, school counselors, and social workers, you will have an ongoing referral source as well as a solid base of professionals to rely on for the many questions you will receive from your members.

Format

By reading the chapters in this book and using the "Something to talk about" questions at the end of each chapter as a basis for discussion, you will have enough material for nine months of meetings (one meeting per month). We recommend the other three meetings each year (one per quarter) include a get-to-know-you activity, a mid-year social for parents and children, and a "Meet the Professionals" panel as described on p.155.

Appendix D

Recommended Reading—From Our Shelf to Yours

Adams, C. (2005) *A Real Boy: A True Story of Autism, Early Intervention and Recovery*. New York: Penguin Group, Inc.

Attwood, T. (1998) *Asperger's Syndrome: A Guide for Parents and Professionals*. London: Jessica Kingsley Publishers.

Baker, J. (2001) *The Autism Social Skills Picture Book*. Arlington, TX: Future Horizons.

Barron, J. and Barron, S. (2002) *There's A Boy in Here*. Arlington, TX: Future Horizons.

Cutler, E. (2004) *Thorn in My Pocket: Temple Grandin's Mother Tells the Family Story*. Arlington, TX: Future Horizons.

Davis, B. and Schunick, W. (2001) *Breaking Autism's Barriers: A Father's Story*. London: Jessica Kingsley Publishers.

Downey, M.K. (2004) *If You've Ever Wanted to Crawl in the Closet with an Oreo: Tips for Parenting a Child with Special Needs*. Euless, TX: Books by MK.

Fouse, B. and Wheeler, M. (1997) *Treasure Chest of Behavioral Strategies for Individuals with Autism*. Arlington, TX: Future Horizons.

Grandin, T. (1995) *Thinking in Pictures and Other Reports from My Life with Autism*. New York: Doubleday.

Greene, R. (2001) *The Explosive Child: A New Approach for Understanding and Parenting Easily Frustrated, Chronically Inflexible Children*. New York: HarperCollins.

Greenfield, J. (1972) *A Child Called Noah: A Family Journey*. New York: Harcourt Brace Jovanovich.

Greenspan, S.I., Wieder, S. and Simons, R. (1998) *The Child with Special Needs: Encouraging Intellectual and Emotional Growth*. New York: Perseus Books.

Haddon, M. (2004) *The Curious Incident of the Dog in the Night-time*. New York: Doubleday.

Hamilton, L.M. (2000) *Facing Autism: Giving Parents Reasons for Hope and Guidance for Help*. Colorado Springs, CO: Waterbrook Press.

Hart, C.A. (1989) *Without Reason: A Family Copes with Two Generations of Autism*. New York: Harper & Row.

Kirby, D. (2005) *Evidence of Harm: Mercury in Vaccines and the Autism Epidemic*. New York: St. Martin's Press.

Koegel, L. and LeZebnik, C. (2004) *Overcoming Autism: Finding the Answers, Strategies, and Hope that Can Transform a Child's Life*. New York: Penguin Group, Inc.

Kranowitz, C.S. (2005) *The Out-of-sync Child: Recognizing and Coping with Sensory Processing Disorder*. New York: Skylight Press.

Kübler-Ross, E. (1969) *On Death and Dying*. New York: Simon & Schuster/Touchstone.

Kübler-Ross, E. (1983) *On Children and Death*. New York: Simon & Schuster/Touchstone.

Lewis, L. (1998) *Special Diets for Special Kids*. Arlington, TX: Future Horizons.

Maurice, C. (1994) *Let Me Hear Your Voice: A Family's Triumph over Autism*. New York: Ballantine Books.

Maurice, C., Green, G. and Luce, S. (1996) *Behavioral Intervention for Young Children with Autism: A Manual for Parents and Professionals*. Austin, TX: Pro-Ed.

McCandless, J. (2003) *Children with Starving Brains: A Medical Treatment Guide for Autism Spectrum Disorder*. New Jersey: Bramble Books.

McKean, T.A. (1994) *Soon Will Come the Light: A View from Inside the Autism Puzzle*. Arlington, TX: Future Horizons.

Neisworth, J.T. and Wolfe, P.S. (eds) (2004) *The Autism Encyclopedia*. Baltimore: Brookes Publishing Company.

Ozonoff, S., Dawson, G. and McPartland, J. (2002) *A Parent's Guide to Asperger Syndrome and High-functioning Autism: How to Meet the Challenges and Help Your Child Thrive*. New York: Guilford Press.

Park, C.C. (1982) *The Siege: A Family's Journey into the World of an Autistic Child*. New York: Little, Brown & Company.

Sparks, N. (2000) *The Rescue*. New York: Warner Books, Inc.

Stacey, P. (2004) *The Boy Who Loved Windows: Opening the Heart and Mind of a Child Threatened with Autism*. Cambridge, MA: Da Copo Press.

Thornburgh, V. and Davie, A.R. (1996) *That All May Worship: An Interfaith Welcome to Persons with Disabilities*. Washington, DC: National Organization on Disability.

Tilton, A.J. (2004) *The Everything Guide to Children with Autism: Know What to Expect, Find the Help You Need, and Get Through the Day*. Holbrook, MA: Adams Media Corporation.

Wilens, T. (1998) *Straight Talk About Psychiatric Medication for Kids*. New York: Guilford Press.

Wright, P.D.W. and Wright, P.D. (2001) *Wrightslaw: From Emotions to Advocacy—The Special Education Survival Guide*. Hartfield, VA: Harbor House Law Press.

Yack, E., Sutton, S. and Aquilla, P. (2003) *Building Bridges through Sensory Integration* (2nd edn). Las Vegas: Sensory Resources.

Index

acceptance, of autism 22, 26, 42, 86, 104, 105
acidophilus 147
adaptation 105
Adderall 48, 88
advocacy, community involvement and awareness activities
  case studies
    Anne and Alex 153–4
    Barbie and John Matthew 154–6
    Dolly 156–9
    Jennifer, Ryan and Kyle 159–61
    Leslie and Jared 161–3
    Nichole and Seth 163–5
    Susan and Mark 165–6
    Susan, Scott and Colton 168–70
    Teresa and Nick 51–2
    Terri and Nicholas 166–8
  professional perspective 170–2
  tip(s)
    Ann's 172
    Anne's 154
    Barbie's 156
    Debbie's 17
    Dolly's 159
    Janis's 19
    Jennifer's 161
    Nicole's 47
    Sonya's 149
    Stacey's 49
    Susan's 166
aggression 52, 53–4, 69, 109, 111–12, 131
anti-seizure medication 48–9
anxiety 129
Applied Behavioral Analysis (ABA)
  case studies 43, 49, 50, 51, 63, 83, 112, 130
  professional perspective 55–6
Asperger's Picnic 155
Asperger's Syndrome
  case studies 15, 22, 31, 73, 84, 103, 123, 154–6, 164, 167
  diagnostic criteria 36–7
  similar disorders 38
assessments 36, 37, 38
Association for Retarded Citizens (Arc) 43, 61
Attention Deficit Disorder (ADD) 84, 148

Attention Deficit Hyperactive Disorder (ADHD) 31, 88, 100, 129, 148
atypical autism 37
audio integration 50
Autism: the Invisible Gift 168
autism
  assessment 37
  checklists 37, 52–3
  diagnostic criteria 36
  explaining to siblings 136
  occurrence 33
  severity 38
  similar disorders 38
Autism Asperger Resource Center (AARC) 170–2
autism awareness activities 51–2
autism service dogs 41–2
Autism Society 170
Autism Society of Hawaii 157
autism-free zones 136–7
Autistic Support Classroom 73
Aware Bear 165
awareness *see* advocacy, community involvement and awareness activities

Behave'n Day 112, 113
behaviors, associated with ASDs 38
bioenergetics assessment 146
biological testing 43
biomedical approach 142–3
Bipolar Disorder 92
Breaking Autism's Barriers: A Father's Story 98
breaks 19
bullying 64–5
business cards 133
Buspar 46

"calm down" spot 46
Camp Determination 172
Carbone method 49
care, of oneself 35, 60
checklists 37, 52–3
cheese 139, 147
chelation 119, 146
Child Development Clinics 165
classical music 50
cognitive ability 37
communication
  professional perspective 81
  sign language 157

201

Do You have a Memorable Story about Your Child?

The stories in this book were shared with us by parents, family members, and professionals who have experienced first-hand the triumphs and trials of living and working with children on the spectrum. If someone in your life is affected with autism, Asperger's Syndrome or PDD and you have a story that will provide hope or encouragement to others in the areas of:

- marriage and family relationships
- faith and religion
- home therapy programs
- humor

we would like to hear from you. Please send your story, including your complete name, address, phone number, and email to diagnosisautism@gmail.com for possible inclusion in an upcoming book.

If you are interested in scheduling a speaking engagement, lecture, seminar, or workshop, please send any inquiries to the same email address.